D1162480

The Advanced Day Planner User's Guide

Hyrum W. Smith

Franklin International Institute, Inc.
Salt Lake City, Utah

Franklin International Institute, Inc.
P.O. Box 25127
Salt Lake City, Utah 84125-0127

Printed in the United States of America

Printing number
7 8 9 10

ISBN 0-939817-01-2

Advantage comes not from the spectacular or the technical. Advantage comes from a persistent seeking of the mundane edge.

—Tom Peters,
A Passion For Excellence

Preface

Kevin L. Hall Vice President, Training and Sales, The Franklin Institute, Inc.

The name Hyrum Smith, while not exactly a household word, is becoming well-known in the field of time management. This reputation is well deserved. In my association with Hyrum, I have grown to love and admire his abilities to teach, communicate warmly with people, and motivate.

Throughout the ten years of our association, I have found Hyrum to be an individual who has the commitment and discipline to do what he says he is going to do. And when it comes to time management, Hyrum practices what he preaches and has motivated thousands of others to do likewise. In compiling the best of those practices in *The Advanced Day Planner User's Guide*, he is providing you with a set of tools that will enhance your abilities to do what you say you are going to do.

I wish all of you could get to know Hyrum as I have. His objective in life is to make a difference in the world. Having helped empower you with the Franklin Day Planner, it is also very important to him to keep you informed and on the cutting edge of personal productivity issues. This book is Hyrum's effort to accomplish these things: to keep in touch with you, the Franklin Day Planner user, and to make a difference in your life.

Introduction

Hyrum W. Smith

At The Franklin Institute, Inc., we receive hundreds of letters every month from Day Planner users. Both in letters and in conversation, I have come to realize that one of the engaging features of the Franklin Day Planner is its adaptability. In speaking with Day Planner users, it is rare when a person does not mention to me some ways he or she has adapted or customized the Planner and, in the process, improved productivity.

The continuing flood of good suggestions tells me that there are many more ways to fine tune personal productivity than we have time to teach in the seminars. This book is the result of my desires to share these ideas with Day Planner users.

Through your use of the Franklin Day Planner, you have already enjoyed a quantum jump in productivity. This book is a collection of improvements, ideas, and helps supplied by those who found that the initial productivity jump merely whetted the appetite. I promise you that applying even a few of the suggestions contained in this book will enhance your productivity and your ability to control events in your life.

Acknowledgments

Many minds have come together to make this book happen. First and foremost I must thank all the Franklin Day Planner users for some terrific ideas, and for the inspiration to write this book. We have received hundreds of suggestions from Day Planner users and have published in this volume only a fraction.

I thank Kurt Hanks for conceiving the idea of the book and for urging me to do it, and Jerry Pulsipher for managing the project. Kurt Hanks, Kathy Stuart, Jean Canestrini, and Kathleen Newman have contributed many hours to make it come together visually. Thanks also to Lisa Vermillion for her patience in carefully editing my chicken scratches. Without any one of these people, I couldn't have done it.

Finally and always, I thank my dear wife and wonderful children for their dedication to my dreams, which allows me to accomplish all I do.

H.W.S.

How To Find What's In This Book

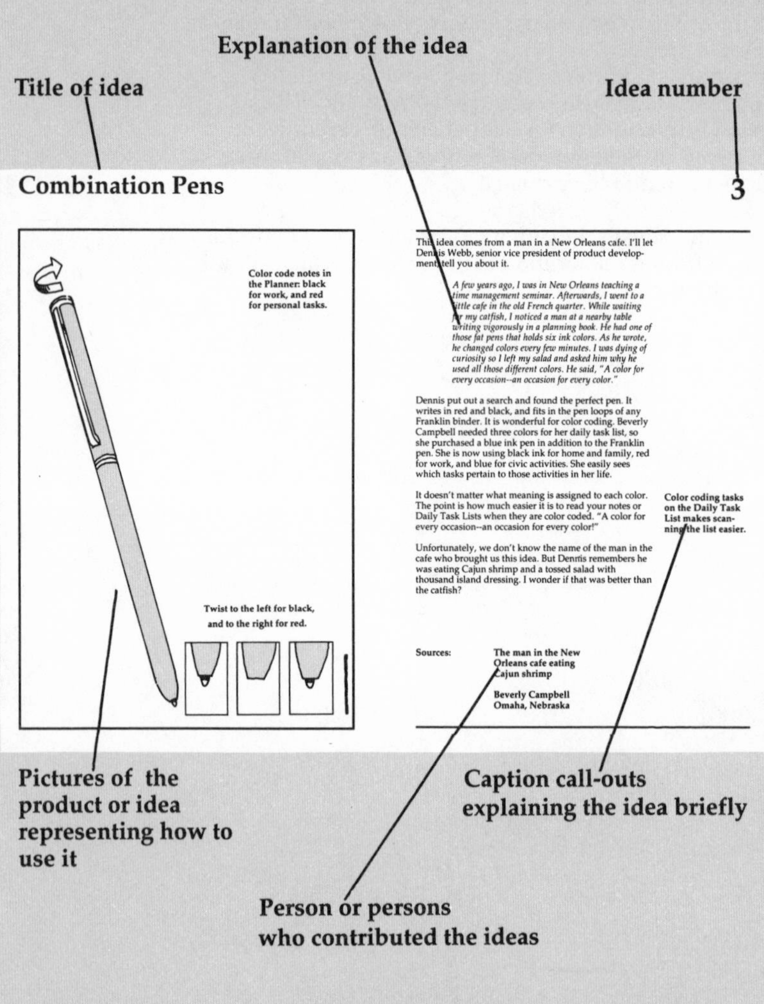

Combination Pens **3**

This idea comes from a man in a New Orleans cafe. I'll let Dennis Webb, senior vice president of product development tell you about it.

A few years ago, I was in New Orleans teaching a time management seminar. Afterwards, I went to a little cafe in the old French quarter. While waiting for my catfish, I noticed a man at a nearby table writing vigorously in a planning book. He had one of those fat pens that holds six ink colors. As he wrote, he changed colors every few minutes. I was dying of curiosity so I left my salad and asked him why he used all those different colors. He said, "A color for every occasion--an occasion for every color."

Dennis put out a search and found the perfect pen. It writes in red and black, and fits in the pen loops of any Franklin binder. It is wonderful for color coding. Beverly Campbell needed three colors for her daily task list, so she purchased a blue ink pen in addition to the Franklin pen. She is now using black ink for home and family, red for work, and blue for civic activities. She easily sees which tasks pertain to those activities in her life.

It doesn't matter what meaning is assigned to each color. The point is how much easier it is to read your notes or Daily Task Lists when they are color coded. "A color for every occasion--an occasion for every color!"

Color coding tasks on the Daily Task List makes scanning the list easier.

Unfortunately, we don't know the name of the man in the cafe who brought us this idea. But Denrtis remembers he was eating Cajun shrimp and a tossed salad with thousand island dressing. I wonder if that was better than the catfish?

Sources: **The man in the New Orleans cafe eating Cajun shrimp**

Beverly Campbell
Omaha, Nebraska

The Advanced Day Planner User's Guide is an idea book. Our objective is to offer a few ideas that will make small but significant improvements in your productivity using the Franklin Day Planner.

Because it is an idea book, we present it in a format easy to scan. Each idea is on a two-page spread—one spread, one idea. The left side is a visual representation of the idea, with captions briefly explaining it. The text is on the right-hand page.

There is a very good reason for this approach. Recent applied research on how the brain processes information shows that there are two sides of the brain: the left side is logical, orderly, and detailed; the right side is creative, intuitive, and holistic. When you look at an object, the two sides of your brain see differently: the left (logical) side scans right, and the right (creative) side scans left. We have laid out this book to appeal to both sides appropriately. The pictures will appeal to your right brain, the text to your left brain. This is all unconscious, of course, and may sound a little corny. But trust me, both halves of your brain will love it!

All that aside, the best way to read this book is to not read it. Thumb through, flip the pages, throw it in the air and let a page fall open—whatever. You don't have to use all the ideas presented. You don't even have to take them all seriously! Just read what interests you. You will probably get the most value from those ideas that appeal to you right off.

If you're looking for a certain topic, don't go to the Table of Contents. There isn't one. But there is a very good Index in the back—try there. The numbers in the Index are not page numbers—there aren't any of those either. Rather, each *idea* is numbered. So, for those of you who value the number of pages in a book, be assured that there are well over 175 here, even though only 83 of them are numbered.

ENJOY!

Subdividing The Daily Task List

By dividing daily tasks into areas of primary concern, you avoid having to "sort through" to find which tasks are appropriate for the moment.

Here are the main tasks for the work day.

Here are the main tasks to accomplish with the family or after work hours.

Here are the goals or values you have decided to work on daily.

When the Daily Task List is full, it's difficult to "sort" through all your tasks to find what can be done right now; some tasks can only be done in the evening, even though they may have a very high priority.

Here are some suggestions:

Joe Blossom divides his Daily Task List into three sections: work, family (and after-hours activities), and values. Throughout the day, he doesn't have to mentally sort the list of things to do at work versus things to do after work. A special place for values gives his day a broader perspective and keeps him focused on those things which are most important in his life.

This is a good way to work those values into tasks you can accomplish today.

Jim Tarchinski was often re-prioritizing, to accommodate new tasks added during the day. He explains his solution:

> *After prioritizing my Daily Task List, I draw a line at the bottom of the list. Then, during the day as I add to the list, I prioritize the additional items. When it's time to begin another task, I look at the items above the line, and compare them to those below the line. The highest priority wins out.*

Avoid re-prioritizing during the day by having two lists: one made during planning and solitude, another made during the day as more tasks surface.

Another user, Bud Wood, reverses codes to distinguish between personal and professional tasks. He designates his work items by A1, A2, B1, B2; and personal items the reverse: 1A, 2A, 1B, 2B.

All of these ideas work—it's a matter of which works best for you. And, of course, there are many more than we have mentioned here. Let your imagination run!

Sources:

Jim Tarchinski
Saginaw, Michigan

Bud Wood
Provo, Utah

Joe Blossom
Syracuse, New York

Corporate Sponsored Planning Sessions

When it was first proposed there were moans and groans of dread.

But when asked if they would like to discontinue it, the staff was unanimous in their opposition.

INDIVIDUAL PLANNING SESSION

First thing in the morning, everyone has an individual planning session for one half hour.

GROUP PLANNING SESSION

Then they meet for a group planning session for another quarter hour.

2

Bob Bennett heard about the following idea:

> *An executive of a small firm told me that all of the people in his company use the Day Planner. This is not unusual, but the way the group utilizes the Day Planner and the concepts taught in the seminar go beyond anything I had heard before.*
>
> *At his company, every morning between 8:00 and 8:30 is spent in individual planning and solitude. Each member of the firm comes in at 8:00, but there are no meetings or other business transactions until 8:30. Everyone is left alone for serious planning of the day's activities.*
>
> *At 8:30, the principals of the firm—each carrying a Franklin Day Planner—gather in the conference room. They discuss the daily tasks that have been given highest priority. Together, they agree on those tasks that are the most important to the company that day. These meetings are usually short—no more than ten minutes—but they provide a sense of direction and unanimity that the firm had not previously enjoyed.*
>
> *This executive told me that there was considerable resistance from his associates when this procedure was first brought up. "Well, let's try it, just to see what happens," the boss suggested. Now, reports my friend, co-workers protest loudly when someone mentions discontinuing the scheduled planning sessions.*

I can't think of a better way to acheive harmony in the workplace and ensure goal-oriented activities than through consistent daily planning and correlation.

Source: **Doug Harris**
Salt Lake City, Utah

Combination Pens

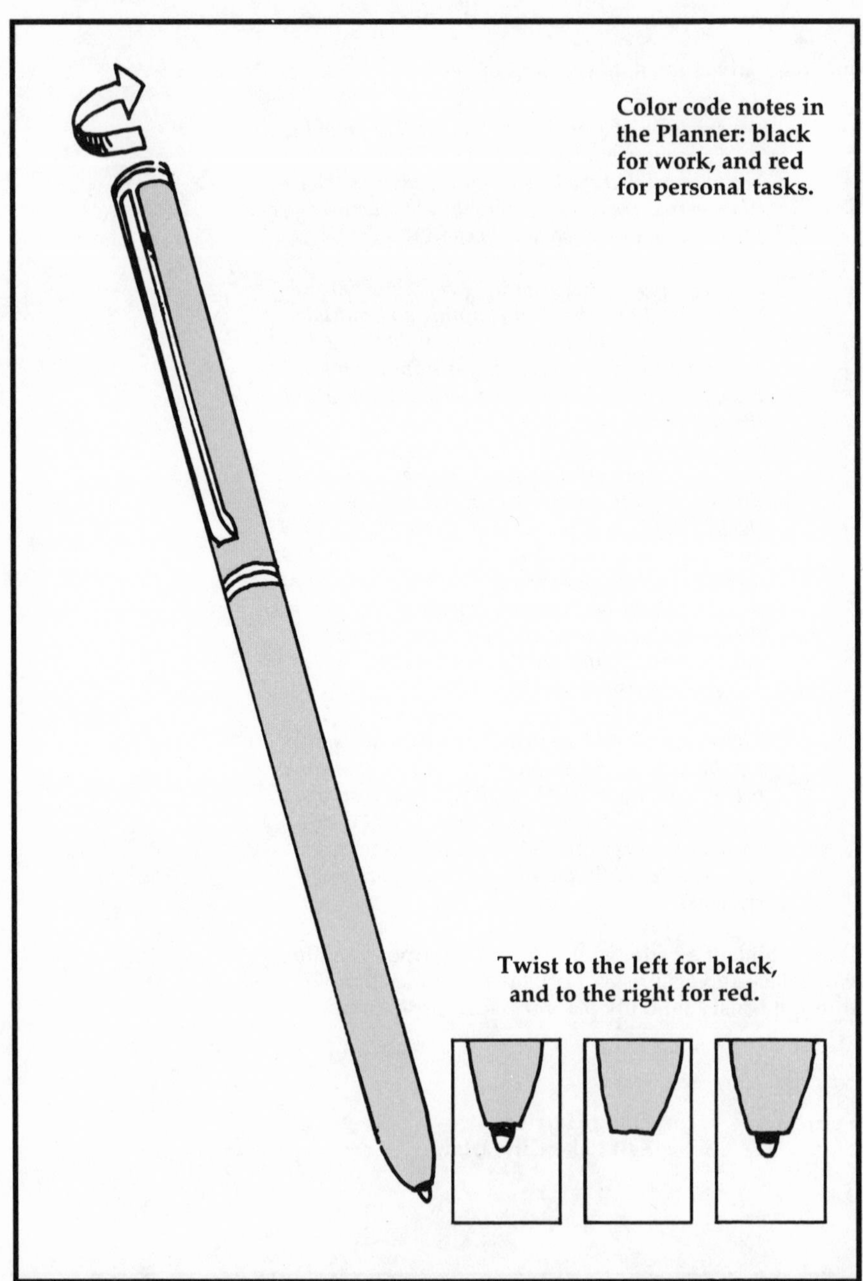

Color code notes in the Planner: black for work, and red for personal tasks.
Twist to the left for black, and to the right for red.

Order No.4030

3

This idea comes from a man in a New Orleans cafe. I'll let Dennis Webb, senior vice president of product development, tell you about it.

> *A few years ago, I was in New Orleans teaching a time management seminar. Afterwards, I went to a little cafe in the old French quarter. While waiting for my catfish, I noticed a man at a nearby table writing vigorously in a planning book. He had one of those fat pens that holds six ink colors. As he wrote, he changed colors every few minutes. I was dying of curiosity so I left my salad and asked him why he used all those different colors. He said, "A color for every occasion—an occasion for every color."*

Dennis put out a search and found the perfect pen. It writes in red and black, and fits in the pen loops of any Franklin binder. It is wonderful for color coding. Beverly Campbell needed three colors for her Daily Task List, so she purchased a blue ink pen in addition to the Franklin pen. She is now using black ink for home and family, red for work, and blue for civic activities. She easily sees which tasks pertain to those activities in her life.

It doesn't matter what meaning is assigned to each color. The point is how much easier it is to read your notes or Daily Task Lists when they are color coded. "A color for every occasion—an occasion for every color!"

Color coding tasks on the Daily Task List makes scanning the list easier.

Unfortunately, we don't know the name of the man in the cafe who brought us this idea. But Dennis remembers he was eating Cajun shrimp and a tossed salad with Thousand Island dressing. I wonder if that was better than the catfish?

Sources:

The man in the New Orleans cafe eating Cajun shrimp

Beverly Campbell
Omaha, Nebraska

Photo and Zipper Pouches

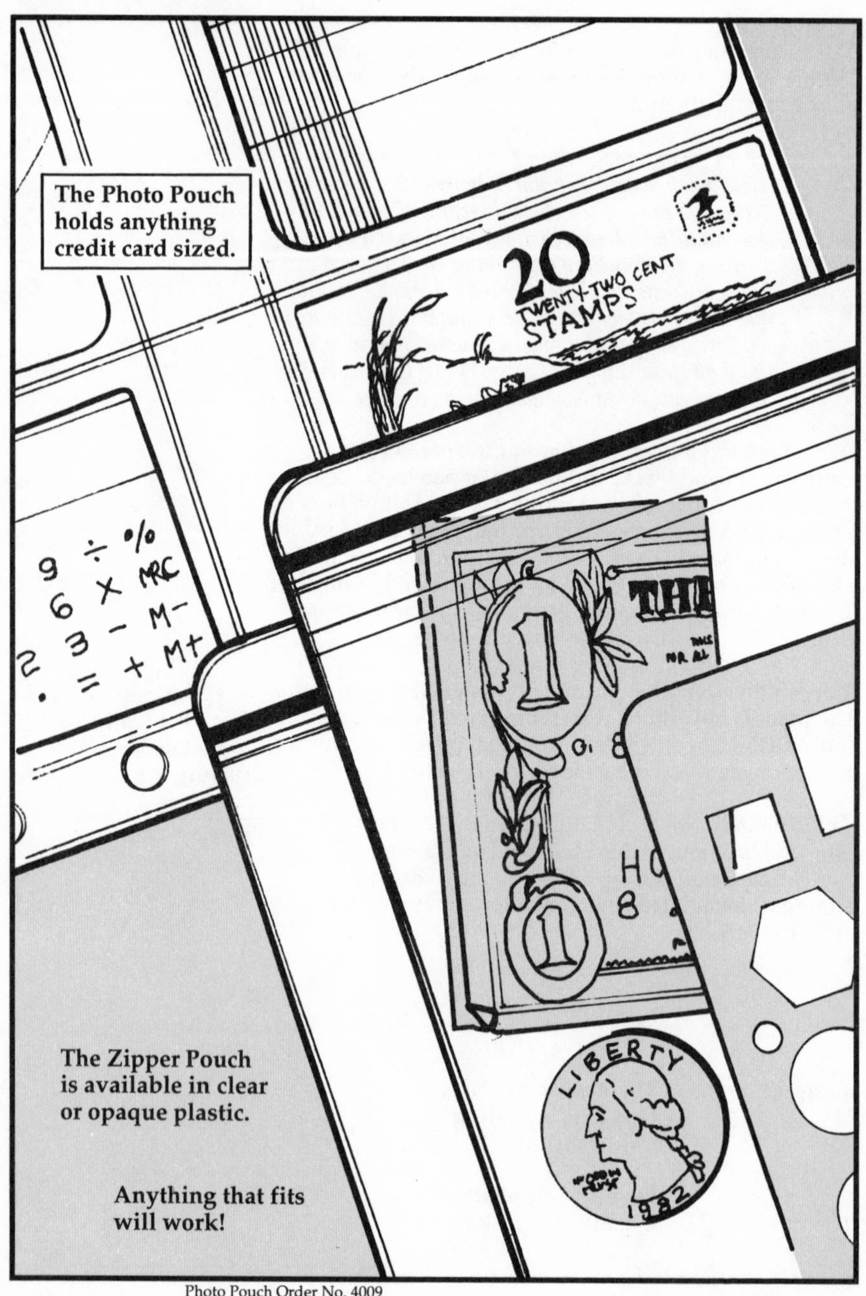
The Photo Pouch holds anything credit card sized.
20
TWENTY-TWO CENT
STAMPS
9 ÷ %
6 × MRC
3 − M−
2
. = + M+
LIBERTY
1982
The Zipper Pouch is available in clear or opaque plastic.
Anything that fits will work!

Photo Pouch Order No. 4009
Zipper Pouch Order No. 4008

These two accessories are for keeping "things" and "stuff" in. The Photo Pouch is designed to hold eight credit cards or photos in each page. The Zipper Pouch is a little like those pencil pouches you used in grade school.

Just for fun, a survey was taken around the office to see how people really use these. Here is a very incomplete list of what can be stored in the Zipper Pouch: money, receipts, calculator, coupons, sewing kit, comb, nail file, Quick Clip (idea 28), aspirin, photos, paper clips, fingernail clippers, rubber bands, parking stickers and validations—shall I go on?

Business cards, highlighter pen, stick of gum (just one—in case of emergency!), razor blade (?), wallpaper and carpet samples, stamps, a template of shapes, labels (idea 61), poems or quotes to memorize, comics, return address labels, unpaid bills, green stamps, spare keys, and computer disks. That's more than my boy Joseph keeps in his pockets!!

Now don't worry, the list for the Photo Pouch isn't nearly as long. Most people keep photos, credit cards, and a Solar Calculator (idea 22). Some other ideas are business cards, spare keys, stamps, hidden money, insurance information, and medical alert cards.

It appears from this list that most people in this office are ready to go on "Let's Make A Deal!"

Source: **The Staff at The Franklin Institute, Inc.**
Salt Lake City, Utah

Boss Updating System

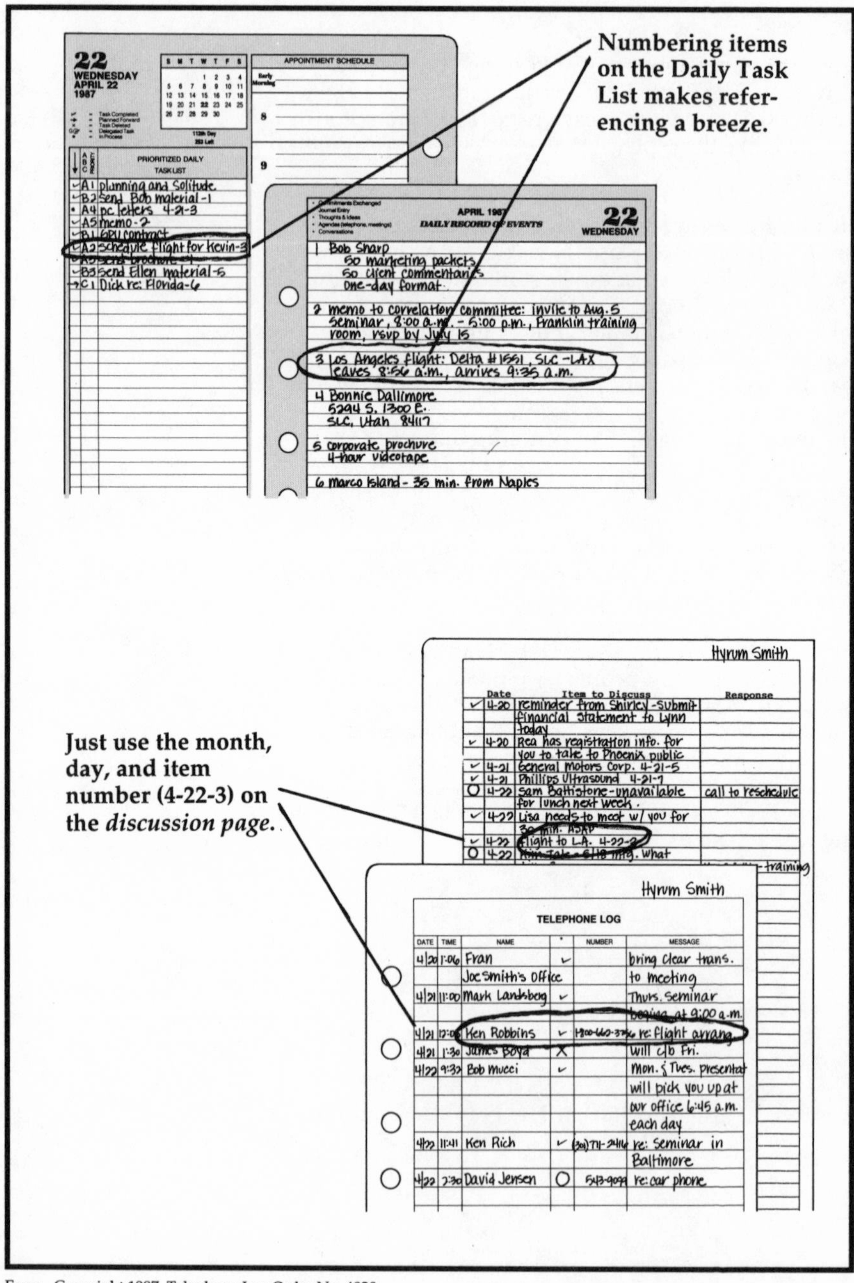

Form Copyright 1987 Telephone Log Order No. 4020

My secretary, Colleen, is a walking phenomenon with the Planner. She keeps my life, and Kevin's, and her family's, and her own in better order than I have ever seen (excepting my wife, in case she's reading this). Since I am out of town more often than not, Colleen must catch me on the run if she needs to talk to me. Here's her version of ultra efficiency:

> *First, every item written on my Daily Record of Events page has a number. (This wasn't my idea—no one seems to know who started it.) On future dates, I refer to items by their numbers. For example, Ruby called from the travel agency on April 22 with information on Hyrum's flight to Los Angeles. She was item number three on my Daily Task List. When I refer to that information, I call it 4-22-3 (April 22, #3).*

No more searching a page of notes for the desired information!

> *I keep one Red Tab for Hyrum and one for Kevin (my other boss). Behind each tab there are at least two pages. One is a Telephone Log, where I record all phone messages. They each receive a copy. The other form is what I call a discussion page. I made this form because I have such limited time with both Hyrum and Kevin. It keeps all items I need to discuss with them in one place.*

A secretary, or anyone, has at hand all items to be discussed with someone, and a record of progress, in one place.

> *Concerning Hyrum's flight, I write on his discussion page the reference number "4-22-3" and a short description, "flight to L.A." I will mention this and a hundred other things to Hyrum when he phones in or is in town. If there is a response or action required, I note it in the response box and use the familiar arrows, dots, and checks to keep track of my progress.*

Colleen is the greatest. I'll tell you, nothing slips through the cracks.

Source: **Colleen Dom**
The Franklin Institute, Inc.
Salt Lake City, Utah

Key Information Section

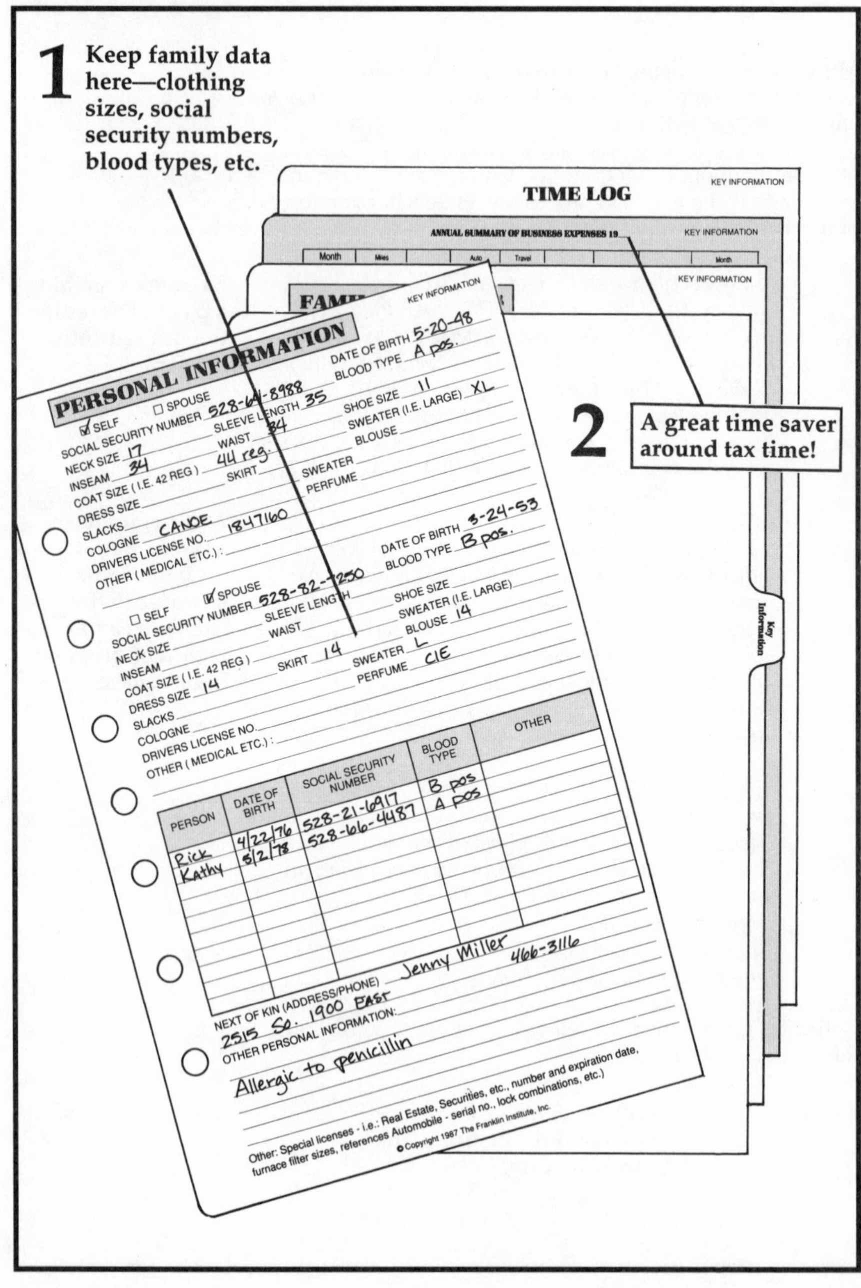

1 Keep family data here—clothing sizes, social security numbers, blood types, etc.
2 A great time saver around tax time!
KEY INFORMATION
TIME LOG
ANNUAL SUMMARY OF BUSINESS EXPENSES 19__
KEY INFORMATION
KEY INFORMATION
PERSONAL INFORMATION
KEY INFORMATION
☑ SELF ☐ SPOUSE
SOCIAL SECURITY NUMBER 528-64-8988
NECK SIZE 17
INSEAM 34
COAT SIZE (I.E. 42 REG)
DRESS SIZE
SLACKS
COLOGNE CANOE
DRIVERS LICENSE NO. 1847160
OTHER (MEDICAL ETC.) :
DATE OF BIRTH 5-20-48
BLOOD TYPE A pos.
SLEEVE LENGTH 35
WAIST 34
44 reg.
SKIRT
SHOE SIZE 11
SWEATER (I.E. LARGE) XL
BLOUSE
SWEATER
PERFUME
☐ SELF ☑ SPOUSE
SOCIAL SECURITY NUMBER 528-82-7250
NECK SIZE
INSEAM
COAT SIZE (I.E. 42 REG)
DRESS SIZE 14
SLACKS
COLOGNE
DRIVERS LICENSE NO.
OTHER (MEDICAL ETC.) :
DATE OF BIRTH 3-24-53
BLOOD TYPE B pos.
SLEEVE LENGTH
WAIST
SKIRT 14
SHOE SIZE
SWEATER (I.E. LARGE)
BLOUSE 14
SWEATER L
PERFUME CIE
PERSON | DATE OF BIRTH | SOCIAL SECURITY NUMBER | BLOOD TYPE | OTHER
Rick | 4/22/76 | 528-21-6917 | B pos
Kathy | 8/2/78 | 528-66-4487 | A pos
NEXT OF KIN (ADDRESS/PHONE) Jenny Miller 466-3116
2515 So. 1900 East
OTHER PERSONAL INFORMATION:
Allergic to penicillin
Other: Special licenses - i.e.: Real Estate, Securities, etc., number and expiration date, furnace filter sizes, references Automobile - serial no., lock combinations, etc.)
© Copyright 1987 The Franklin Institute, Inc.
Key Information

Where do you keep your spouse's social security number, or the emergency phone number for your credit cards? If you said the Key Information section, that's right! Key Information is a personal reference section that is always with you and easy to find.

Personal information goes on the first page: social security numbers, clothing sizes, driver's license numbers, etc. There is also an information chart for others, including birth date, social security number, and blood type.

The next page is for credit and financial information. There is a place for account numbers and for toll-free phone numbers to report thefts or problems. All family advisors are listed on the following page: doctors, dentist, insurance agents, financial advisors, etc. The page entitled Notes could include dimensions of your home and properties, special medical data, boat or RV information—anything you may need to refer to. And, by the way, the 1988 Planner will include a Gift List page and a Gift Ideas page.

The Annual Summary of Business Expenses is on the following page. This is especially useful around tax season! At the bottom on the back side of this page is the Automobile Information and Servicing Record. Quick! When was the last time you had the oil changed? Don't feel bad if you don't know—few people do. Lynn Robbins records the cost of every repair in this space. At the end of the year he has a complete annual auto maintenance record, particularly useful for budgeting the following year.

We created these forms based on what WE thought you may need. If your needs are different, create your own form, and send us a copy. We may include it in *The Advanced Day Planner User's Guide, Volume II!*

Source: **Lynn G. Robbins**
The Franklin Institute, Inc.
Salt Lake City, Utah

Action Files

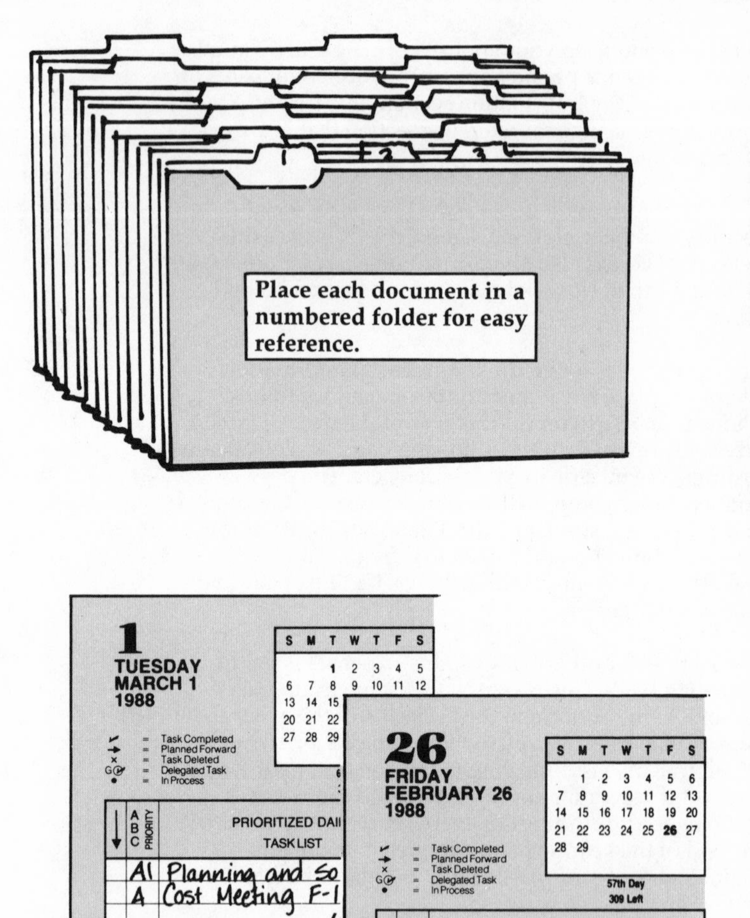

Every time you need to refer to that document (for a future task or event), note the folder number in your Planner.

This is a simple way to reference from your Planner to documents in other files. Roy Vining writes:

> *A co-worker of mine made the suggestion about how to keep up with papers you receive that need short-term action (within a couple of weeks) but cannot be handled immediately. Begin with folders labeled 1-25. When a meeting notice and agenda comes to me today for a meeting on March 1, I put it in the first available folder (F-1). Then in my Planner on March 1, I write "Cost Meeting F-1." This tells me to take this folder to the meeting with me. If I need to prepare an agenda item by February 26, I write "F-1" by that task also. This method supersedes my "For Action" folder into which 20-25 such items were placed; when something was needed, I had to sort through the whole folder. This new system is working well for me.*

Organizes documents.

Eliminates paper shuffling.

Source: **Roy Vining**
Dow Chemical Co.
Freeport, Texas

A Source of Documentation

One of the great things about the Franklin Day Planner is it gets us in the habit of documenting everything that happens during the day. The Planner actually can be used as proof and documentation of events, and has been used in court as evidence!

When Don Barkley was involved in a two-car collision, he wrote down everything that happened, who was involved, and visible damage to each vehicle. Later, when they went to court, Don submitted the information in his Day Planner as proof of what happened. The judge awarded him the case based largely on that evidence.

Keeping good records in the Planner can save you money and frustration when it is necessary to retrace your steps.

Joan DeMille sells for a large real estate company. She had been working for months with a woman to negotiate a price on a house. Finally, the client herself contacted the owners and negotiated a price. Reluctant to pay the commission fees, the client went to Joan's office and reported to the office manager that her calls were never returned and that Joan was not helpful in selling the home. When Joan's boss called her into the office, he reprimanded her for her negligence. Joan opened her Day Planner and showed her boss, from her Daily Task Lists and Daily Record of Events pages, all the calls (long distance) she had made to the client in trying to arrange the sale. The fact that she was able to prove her contacts with the client meant $25,000 in commissions for the company.

What if Howard Hughes had kept a Planner?

You may never need to take your Day Planner to court with you, and it may never save your job. But just think what we would know now if Howard Hughes had only recorded more in his Planner . . .

Source: **Don Barkley**
Dallas, Texas

Joan DeMille
Detroit, Michigan

Follow-Up Reminder

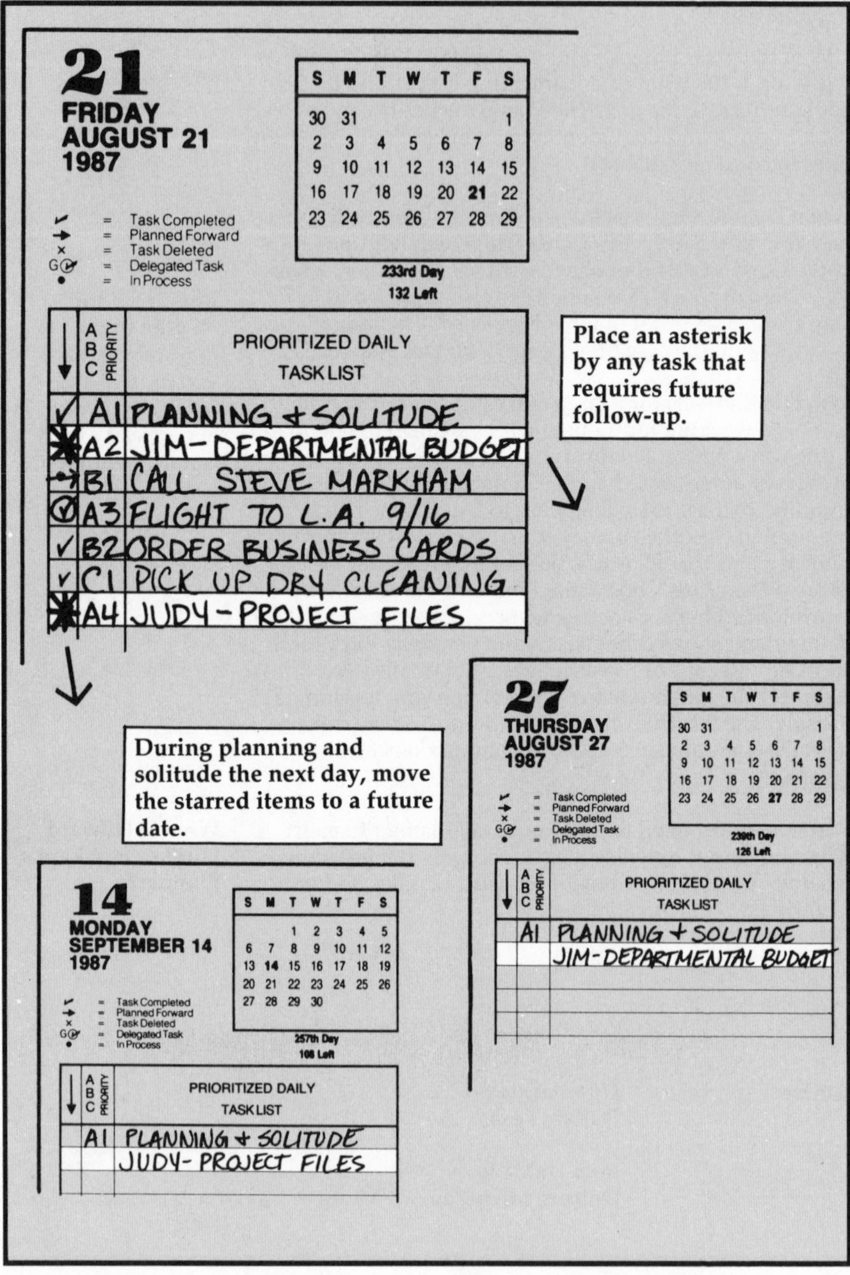

21
FRIDAY
AUGUST 21
1987
S M T W T F S
30 31 1
2 3 4 5 6 7 8
9 10 11 12 13 14 15
16 17 18 19 20 21 22
23 24 25 26 27 28 29
= Task Completed
= Planned Forward
= Task Deleted
G = Delegated Task
= In Process
233rd Day
132 Left
PRIORITIZED DAILY TASK LIST
A1 PLANNING + SOLITUDE
A2 JIM-DEPARTMENTAL BUDGET
B1 CALL STEVE MARKHAM
A3 FLIGHT TO L.A. 9/16
B2 ORDER BUSINESS CARDS
C1 PICK UP DRY CLEANING
A4 JUDY-PROJECT FILES
Place an asterisk by any task that requires future follow-up.
During planning and solitude the next day, move the starred items to a future date.
27
THURSDAY
AUGUST 27
1987
239th Day
126 Left
A1 PLANNING + SOLITUDE
JIM-DEPARTMENTAL BUDGET
14
MONDAY
SEPTEMBER 14
1987
257th Day
108 Left
A1 PLANNING + SOLITUDE
JUDY-PROJECT FILES

Many completed tasks that have earned checks in the Daily Task List require follow-up action. But if it isn't written down right away, the follow-up task may be forgotten.

Charles Sewell puts an asterisk (*) by any task that needs future follow-up. Later, during planning and solitude, he moves the required notes to a future date and checks off the asterisk. This way, he is reminded not only that follow-up is required, but also that it must be planned forward to a future date.

Anne Summers, a secretary, used to forget follow-up tasks in her Planner because she didn't write them down immediately. Every few weeks she reviewed her past Daily Task Lists for any forgotten tasks—and invariably found some. I showed her this letter from Charles and now she is doing much better. She said an asterisk bothers her to action even more than an arrow!

Source: **Charles Sewell**
Dow Chemical
Freeport, Texas

Anne Summers
Salt Lake City, Utah

Suspense File

Note the name of the client to be called in the Daily Task List.

14
MONDAY
SEPTEMBER 14
1987

S	M	T	W	T	F	S
		1	2	3	4	5
6	7	8	9	10	11	12
13	14	15	16	17	18	19
20	21	22	23	24	25	26
27	28	29	30			

257th Day
108 Left

✓ = Task Completed
→ = Planned Forward
x = Task Deleted
G = Delegated Task
• = In Process

↓	ABC	PRIORITY	PRIORITIZED DAILY TASK LIST
			Jack Dobson-Acme-PE

PROSPECT FILE

Company Acme Construction Date 11-9-87
Name of Contact Jack Dobson Title Sr. V.P.
Address Tel. No.
Tel. No.
Comments 400 Employees
Source of Lead Dave Date Received 11-7-87
Best Time To Call 9:00 Eastern

Date Con-tacted	Type of Contact: Person	Phone	Other	Response	Follow Up Date
11/9		✓		Interested-send info.	11/23

Prospect Rating A-Excellent B-Good C-Marginal A

A

Instead of physically moving client cards to a dated file, keep an alphabetized file.

10

Follow-up is a crucial part of every project. A suspense file is a common way to track follow-up, particularly in sales. When a client says, "Call me in three weeks," the client's card is placed in a dated tickler file under the date the call should be made. But if the client calls in two weeks, where is the card? Nobody knows. If you can't remember anything about the client and can't find his card, you're in big trouble. You may lose the sale.

The goal is to have all information retrievable at any time, quickly and easily. Wouldn't that improve sales? With The Franklin Day Planner it's fairly simple.

Begin with a Prospect File. Make one page for each client and alphabetize the file. If there are only a few pages in the file, store them in the Planner; if there are many, use an extra binder. When the client says, "Call me in three weeks," note in your Day Planner three weeks from today to call Client A, and make reference to the Prospect File ("PF").

Save time and frustration when the client calls unexpectedly.

When Client A calls unexpectedly in two weeks, the document is still in the Prospect File under A—you always know where it is. On any given day, you will have staring up at you, during planning and solitude, the names of several clients. Will you forget to call them? No. Will you put off those calls? Not likely—they earn either checks or arrows. Do you know how it feels to arrow ten tasks from one day? I wouldn't recommend it.

Try this system for one month, and you will never go back to card shuffling again.

Source: **The Marketing Department**
The Franklin Institute, Inc.
Salt Lake City, Utah

Franklin Binders

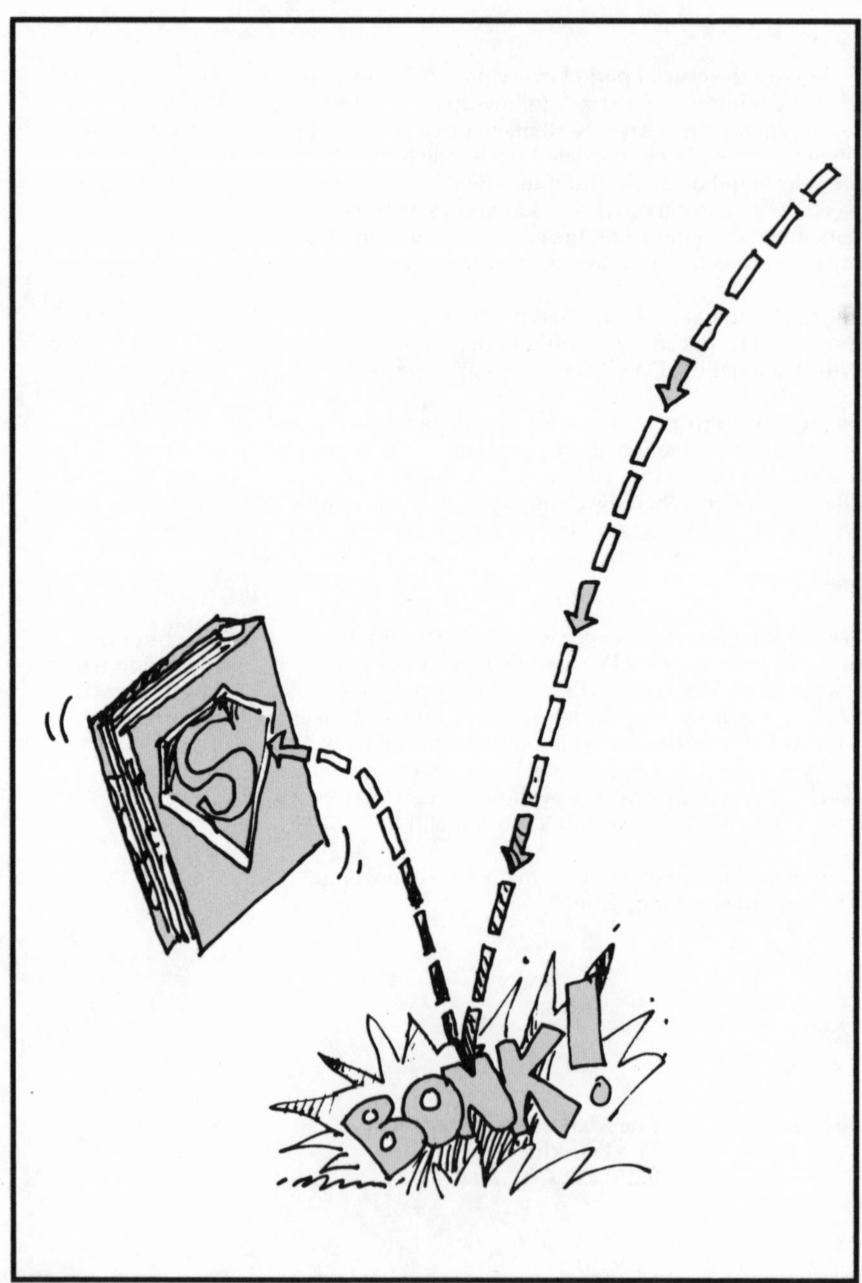

Everyone has heard of the watch that "takes a licking and keeps on ticking." But I'll bet Franklin binders take more hard knocks than any watch.

Richard Stroebel likes the fine padding in our leather binders—he says it makes an ideal pillow for a noontime nap!

One of the more popular tricks of Franklin Planner users is leaving the Planner on the roof of the car and driving off. (This is particularly interesting when it's raining.) One man ran over his own Planner in his driveway. He reported that the hardware was smashed, but the simulated leather survived without a scratch. That's durability!

Many styles and varieties of binders for your Franklin Day Planner are available.

My favorite story is about the Philadelphia man who was met by an armed mugger on the way home from work one night. By chance, he had left his wallet at work that day. I guess that upset the mugger because he fired a shot as he ran away. The bullet hit the man's Planner, and he was saved—it didn't even go through all the pages! (They don't really expect me to believe that story, do they?)

Warning! Do not try any of these stunts at home—you may endanger your Day Planner!

Source: **Richard Stroebel**
USG
Saginaw, Michigan

Correspondence

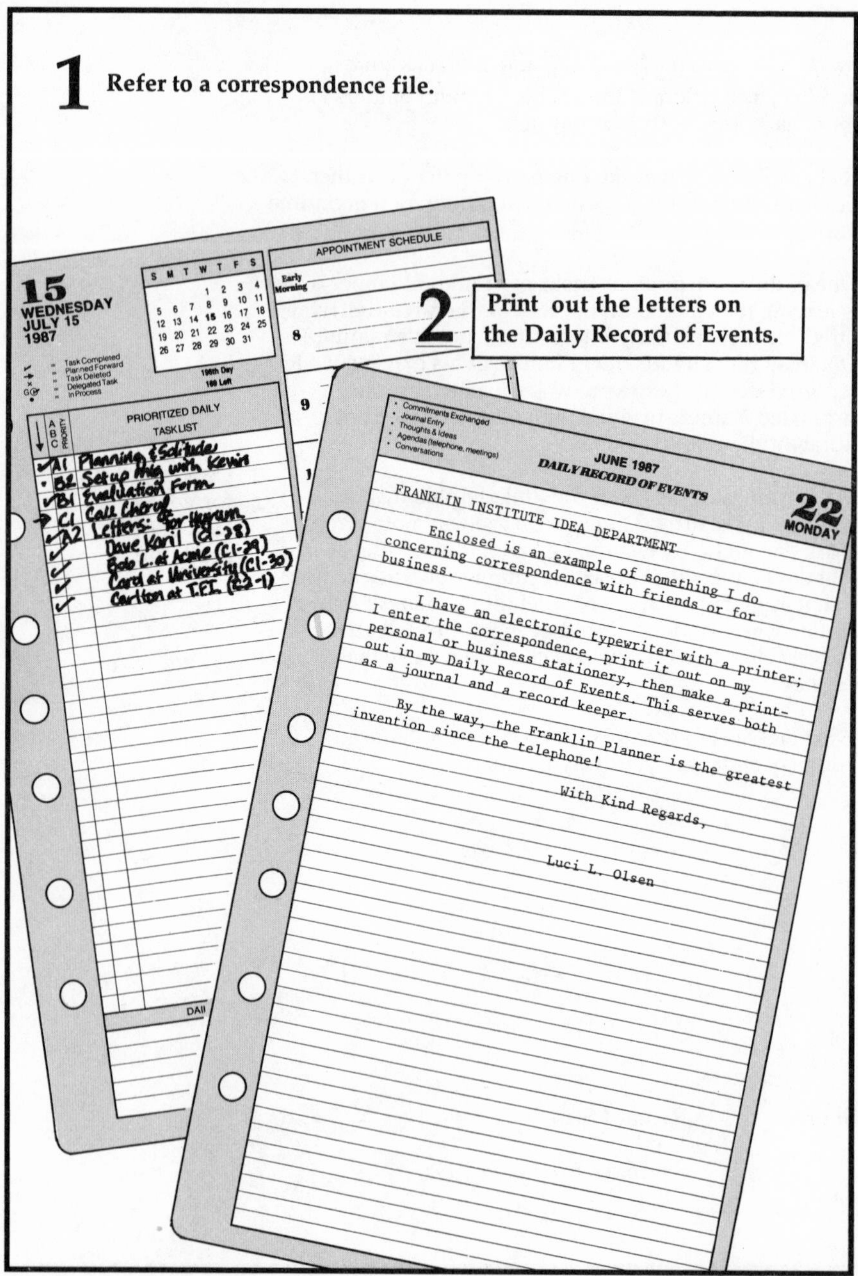

1 Refer to a correspondence file.
15
WEDNESDAY
JULY 15
1987
APPOINTMENT SCHEDULE
PRIORITIZED DAILY
TASKLIST
A1 Planning & Solitude
B2 Set up Mtg with Kevin
B1 Evaluation Form
C1 Call Cheryl
A2 Letters: for Hyrum
Dave Karil (C1-28)
Bob L. at Acme (C1-29)
Carol at University (C1-30)
Carlton at T.F.I. (C2-1)
2 Print out the letters on the Daily Record of Events.
JUNE 1987
DAILY RECORD OF EVENTS
22
MONDAY
FRANKLIN INSTITUTE IDEA DEPARTMENT
Enclosed is an example of something I do concerning correspondence with friends or for business.
I have an electronic typewriter with a printer; I enter the correspondence, print it out on my personal or business stationery, then make a print-out in my Daily Record of Events. This serves both as a journal and a record keeper.
By the way, the Franklin Planner is the greatest invention since the telephone!
With Kind Regards,
Luci L. Olsen

Luci Olsen shared with us her idea concerning correspondence with friends or business associates.

> *I have an electronic typewriter with a printer; I enter the correspondence, print it out on my personal or business stationery, then make a printout in my Daily Record of Events. This serves both as a journal and a record keeper.*
>
> *By the way, the Franklin Planner is the greatest invention since the telephone!*

Colleen Dom does most of my business correspondence. Since there is too much to keep in her Planner, she keeps files according to client company. When she needs to type a letter, the task goes in her Daily Task List. She types the letter, then makes a copy and gives it a number. The copy goes in the correspondence file, and the number goes in her Daily Task List next to that task. If she needs to backtrack, the numbers send her to the correct file, and the letter's place in the file.

Sources: **Luci Olsen**
Young Ward, Utah

Colleen Dom
The Franklin Institute, Inc.
Salt Lake City, Utah

The Franklin Day Planner And the Computer

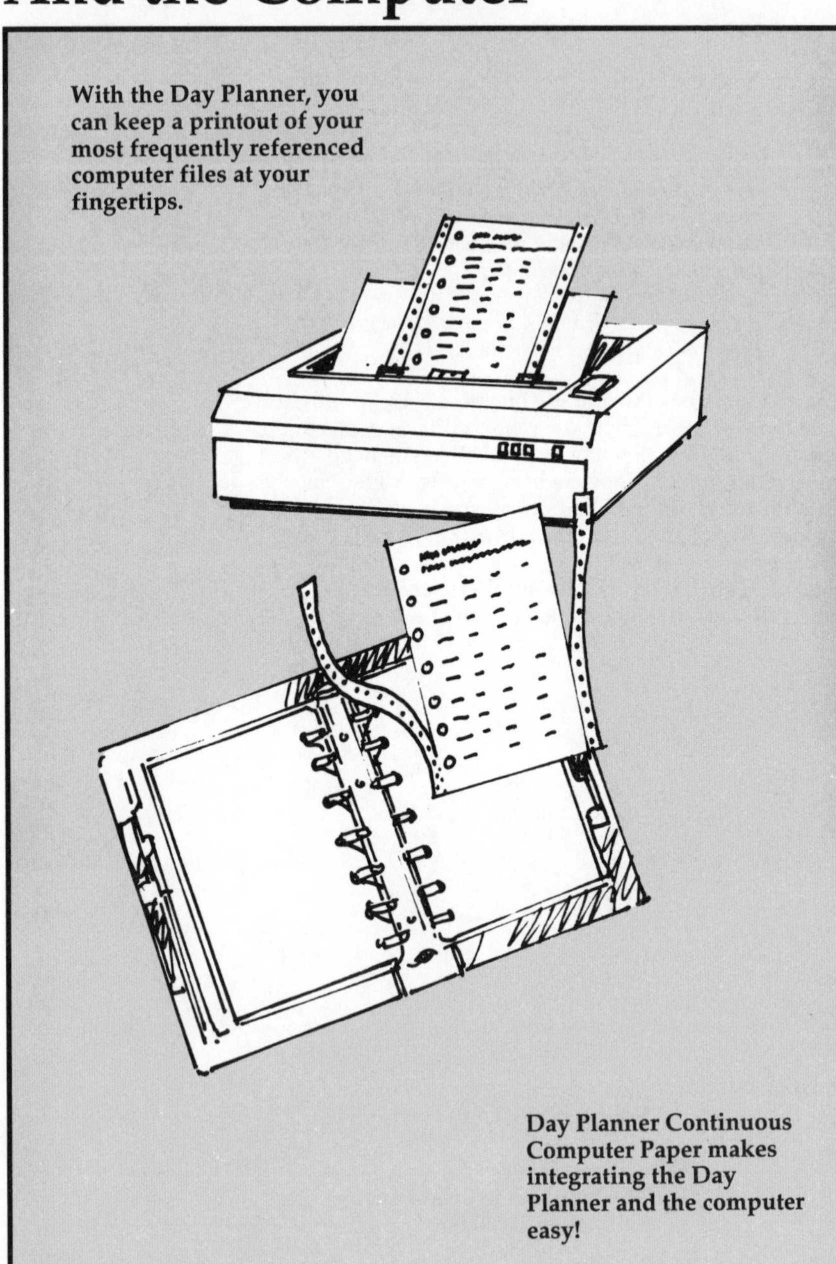

With the Day Planner, you can keep a printout of your most frequently referenced computer files at your fingertips.
Day Planner Continuous Computer Paper makes integrating the Day Planner and the computer easy!

The Franklin Day Planner keeps information at your fingertips. The computer offers quick access and massive storage capabilities. These tools together can work very effectively to help you be more productive.

Because of the faster sorting and figuring capabilities, many people use personal computers for financial records. Checking accounts, savings accounts, and securities can all be tracked by computer, and the balance is figured automatically.

The computer is a great place to store a master prospect or client file. In order for it to work effectively, you must have a computer at your desk. When on the phone with a client, input information as you talk. Before leaving on sales calls, print out the files needed on Franklin's Continuous Computer Paper so that you have the necessary information with you. Back at the office, input any notes taken at the meeting.

Values and goals often change from what we originally thought; on computer they are easily edited. Keep a printout in your Planner for reference during planning and solitude.

Project management is easily tracked by computer. Deadlines and assignments are quickly edited. Again, keep a copy in the Planner for reference.

The computer can be a valuable companion to the Franklin Planner. But beware of double entry; taking notes in the Planner, then updating files on the computer can be very time-consuming. Before deciding to keep a file on computer, evaluate whether it will really save time and effort.

Source: **Karl M. Hillyard**
The Franklin Institute, Inc.
Salt Lake City, Utah

Delegation Form

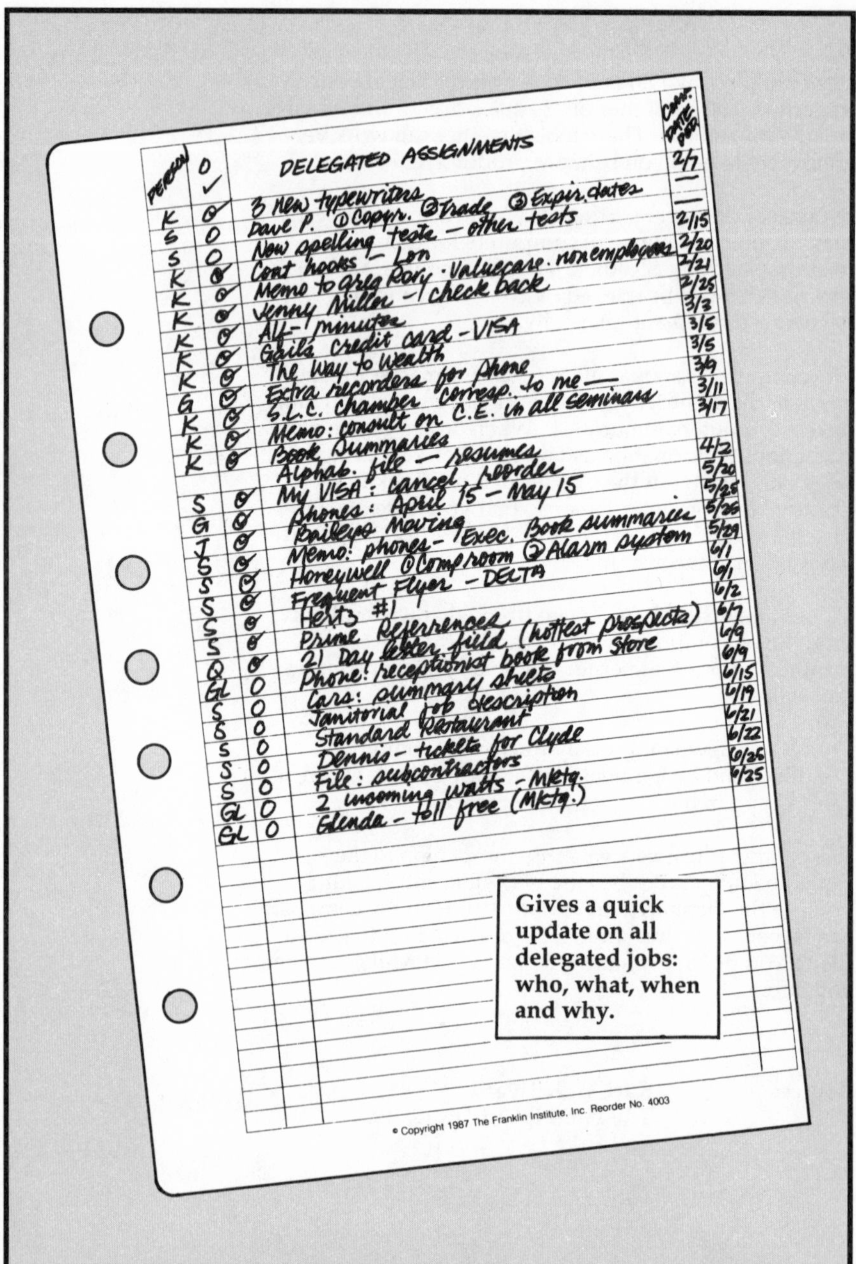

PERSON	O ✓	DELEGATED ASSIGNMENTS	COMP. DATE DUE 2/7
K	✓	3 New typewriters	—
S	O	Dave P. ① Copyr. ② Trade ③ Expir. dates	—
S	O	New spelling tests — other tests	2/15
K	✓	Coat hooks — Lon	2/20
K	✓	Memo to Greg Rory · Valuecare · nonemployees	2/21
K	✓	Jenny Miller — I check back	2/25
K	✓	All — minutes	3/3
K	✓	Gail's credit card — VISA	3/5
K	✓	The Way to Wealth	3/5
K	✓	Extra recorders for phone	3/9
G	✓	S.L.C. chamber corresp. to me —	3/11
K	✓	Memo: consult on C.E. in all seminars	3/17
K	✓	Book Summaries	
K	✓	Alphab. file — resumes	4/2
S	✓	My VISA: cancel, reorder	5/20
G	✓	Phones: April 15 — May 15	5/25
J	✓	Baileys Moving	5/26
S	✓	Memo: phones — Exec. Book summaries	5/29
S	✓	Honeywell ① Comp room ② Alarm system	6/1
S	✓	Frequent Flyer — DELTA	6/1
S	✓	Hertz #1	6/2
S	✓	Prime References	6/7
Q	✓	21 Day letter field (hottest prospects)	6/9
GL	O	Phone: receptionist book from store	6/9
S	O	Cars: summary sheets	6/15
S	O	Janitorial job description	6/19
S	O	Standard Restaurant	6/21
S	O	Dennis — tickets for Clyde	6/22
S	O	File: subcontractors	6/25
GL	O	2 incoming watts — Mktg.	6/25
GL	O	Glenda — toll free (Mktg.)	

Gives a quick update on all delegated jobs: who, what, when and why.

14

Lynn Robbins, senior vice president at Franklin, delegates many tasks that don't have a route in time. He used to note these tasks in the Prioritized Daily Task List many times, and arrow them several times during the month. Now he records them all on a Delegation Form. This form, his own creation, outlines the delegated task and person responsible, and eliminates for Lynn the need to arrow forward many times on a single task. The task is arrowed once to the Delegation Form; then he reviews the form periodically to check progress on these assignments.

For example, Lynn asked Shirley, his secretary, to check on his Frequent Flyer status with Delta Airlines. He told her, when he gave her the task, that it was low priority—to do it when she got the chance. Shirley recorded it in her Planner as low priority for Lynn. A week later, she reported back to Lynn what she had found out; he checked off the task on the Delegation Form and recorded the information on the Daily Record of Events.

Lynn has enjoyed having in one place a progress report of those delegated tasks that have no deadline. It reduces arrowing and writing in tasks on Daily Task Lists, and makes review much simpler.

Source: **Lynn G. Robbins**
Senior Vice President
The Franklin Institute, Inc.

Photocopying Forms

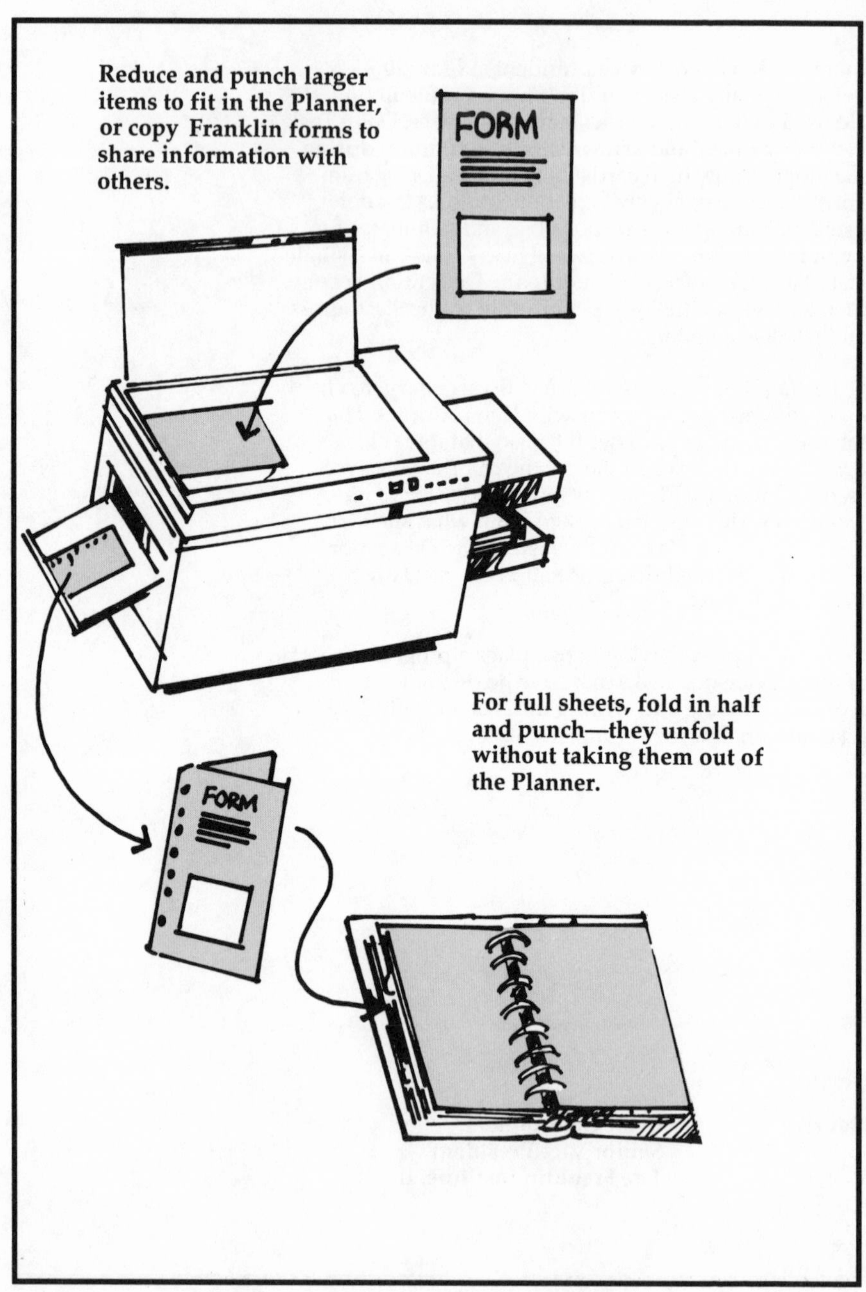

Reduce and punch larger items to fit in the Planner, or copy Franklin forms to share information with others.
FORM
For full sheets, fold in half and punch—they unfold without taking them out of the Planner.
FORM

Photocopiers are wonderful machines, if you can get them to work. In our office, we copy almost everything to fit in the Planner. So we make sure that our copiers handle at least two sizes of paper, and we keep our seven-hole punched Blank Paper in one bin all the time.

There is a wonderful guy named Tom Young who owns Young Electric Sign Company in Salt Lake City. I say he's wonderful because he has converted almost everyone he knows, and many he doesn't know, to the Franklin Day Planner. Tom has learned the value of a photocopier. He explains:

> *If I am to see an individual who has written me a letter, I place a reduced copy of the letter, cut and punched, into the proper date and it acts as a reminder, a tickler file, and certainly a wonderful ready reference when I finally meet that person face-to-face.*

What a great idea! I wonder why I didn't think of it.

Any forms available on Day Planner paper can be copied for future reference and for sharing the information with others: Travel Itineraries, Meeting Agendas, project files, graphs—anything you want someone else to see.

Letter-sized pages fit nicely in the Planner also. Lisa Vermillion simply folds them in half and punches near the fold line. When the Planner is open to one of these pages, she can unfold it without removing it from the Planner.

Sources: **Tom Young**
Young Electric Sign Company
Salt Lake City, Utah

Lisa Vermillion
The Franklin Institute, Inc.
Salt Lake City, Utah

Evaluating Your Daily Task List

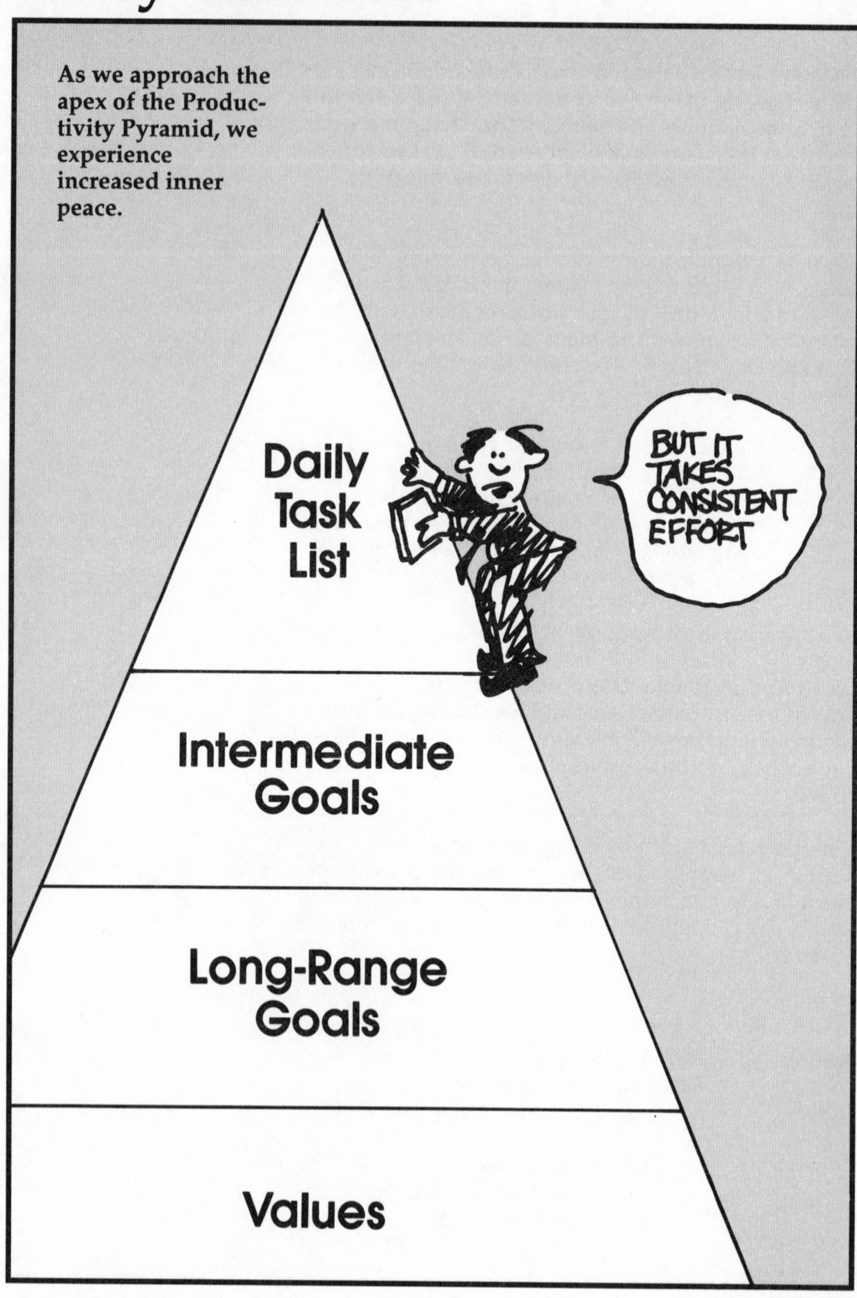

16

Arrowing several tasks from one day feels lousy. Why? It may have nothing to do with how effectively we use our time. But it may indicate other things. Eugene Fischer explains:

> *The Franklin method is a vast improvement over the "to do" list which I have attempted from time to time. Each day it forces me to set priorities and allows me to assess how effective I was in following my plan. So far, I find that I plan a lot more than I accomplish. As long as I maintain an awareness of that fact, I will be motivated to seek an answer to the question, "Is my plan unrealistic, or do I need to find ways to improve effectiveness?"*

High productivity has little to do with sheer volume of tasks completed each day.

That question is key to finding the apex (the point of highest productivity) of our Personal Productivity Pyramid. Worrying about too many tasks for one day overwhelms and hinders us. If that seems to be your pattern, begin evaluating on a daily basis, as Eugene recommends. Some other helpful questions are:

- What is the long-range priority of this project?
- For whom am I doing this task? When do they need it?
- What can I delegate?
- Is this urgency more important than another priority?
- Are any of the A's or B's really C's?
- What will happen if I wait on this task? (The answer to this question will have significant bearing on the task's priority.)
- Can I delete any tasks?
- Have I included time for myself and my family?
- Are any of these tasks infringing on my values?

When you feel overwhelmed by your Daily Task List, ask some of these evaluating questions.

Remember, as we approach the apex of our Pyramid, we experience greater inner peace. When we feel ourselves drifting further from that, it's time to evaluate.

Source: **Eugene M. Fischer**
Swenson Anderson Associates
Minneapolis, Minnesota

Company Manuals

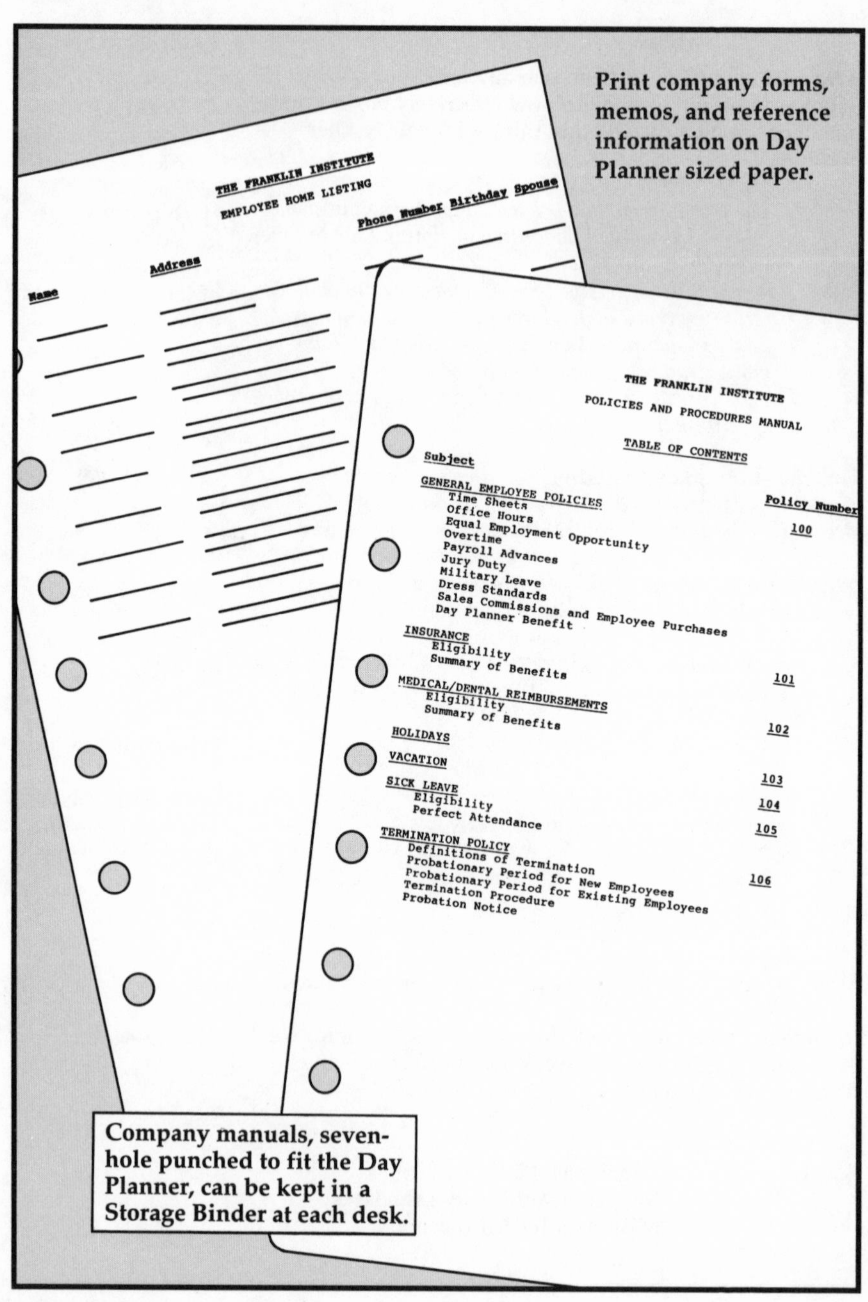

Dow Chemical has trained literally thousands of employees across the world on the Franklin Day Planner. Consequently, they can easily standardize company forms and correspondence to fit the Day Planner. One division of Dow prints their Mission Statement on Day Planner paper. Every employee has ready access to the information and knows where to find it.

At Franklin, we print memos, forms, and reference information on Day Planner paper: seminar dates and locations, product price lists, an employee phone directory, travel expense reports, etc.

In this book, you will see many forms that users have made themselves. If you would like some of your original forms printed, there is a Custom Forms Department at the Franklin Institute.

Having all forms and manuals standardized to fit the Day Planner makes life easier. Important information is less likely to be tossed into a bottomless stack of papers, because the seven holes punched in the document are an invitation to make it a part of your life!

Source: **Dow Chemical**

Setting Goals With Employees

The successful manager is willing to do that which the unsuccessful manager is not willing to do. Among other things, an effective manager sets goals with employees. Goal setting *with* an employee rather than *for* an employee can make all the difference in morale, motivation, and, therefore, productivity.

Keep one goal sheet for each employee—track goals, tasks, deadlines.

Bryon Johnson, postmaster, meets regularly with each of his employees to negotiate goals and deadlines. The frequency of meetings depends on the specific goal, but he meets no more than once a week and no less than every six months with each employee. They discuss problems, identify needs, and agree upon courses of action in the form of goals. After prioritizing the goals, they break them down into smaller tasks, each with a deadline. Both parties are involved in the whole process and must agree on decisions made.

For follow-up—and because a goal not written is only a wish—he uses a goal sheet for each employee, on which he records the goals and tracks progress on intermediate goals and deadlines. He finds these written records helpful in many ways, especially when it is time to evaluate performance.

Extra Values and Goals sheets are available in packages of 50.

This is also a valuable exercise for families; it provides an opportunity to meet with each child individually, to discuss what is most important to him or her.

I think you'll find a marked difference in morale, whether among employees or family members, when individuals are consulted on a regular basis to contribute to their own and an organization's goals.

Source: **Bryon L. Johnson**
Postmaster
Park City, Utah

Indexing

INFORMATION

TAB

A–C

Christmas Card List

Phone

D–F

Employee Info.

Red 1

G–J

Key Info

Jan

K–M

Red 5

Kids - Gift Ideas

Red 4

Meeting Agendas

N–P

V+G

Personality Profile

Key Info.

Perfume (Jan)

Q–S

Index alphabetically or by tab. Make your index easy to edit.

19

"I know it's in here somewhere. I filed it in my Planner just last week—but where?" Sound familiar? Lynn Robbins was going through that routine a little too often, so he made an index to his Planner.

Lynn's index is a table of contents for the entire tabbed section of his Planner. His Christmas card list is filed with the blue Address and Phone section. A personality profile is under the Values and Goals tab. His wife's favorite perfume is written in the Key Information section. Employee information is under Red Tab #1, and Meeting Agendas are all kept in Red Tab #4.

There is a wealth of information stored in the tabbed sections. Thumbing page by page to find certain information, says Lynn, is like trying to find your child at an amusement park on a Saturday—it takes too much time, and you'll see a lot of kids before you find the one you're looking for.

Index all information kept in the tabbed sections of the Planner to prevent "losing" details.

Source: **Lynn Robbins**
The Franklin Institute, Inc.
Salt Lake City, Utah

Bill Payments

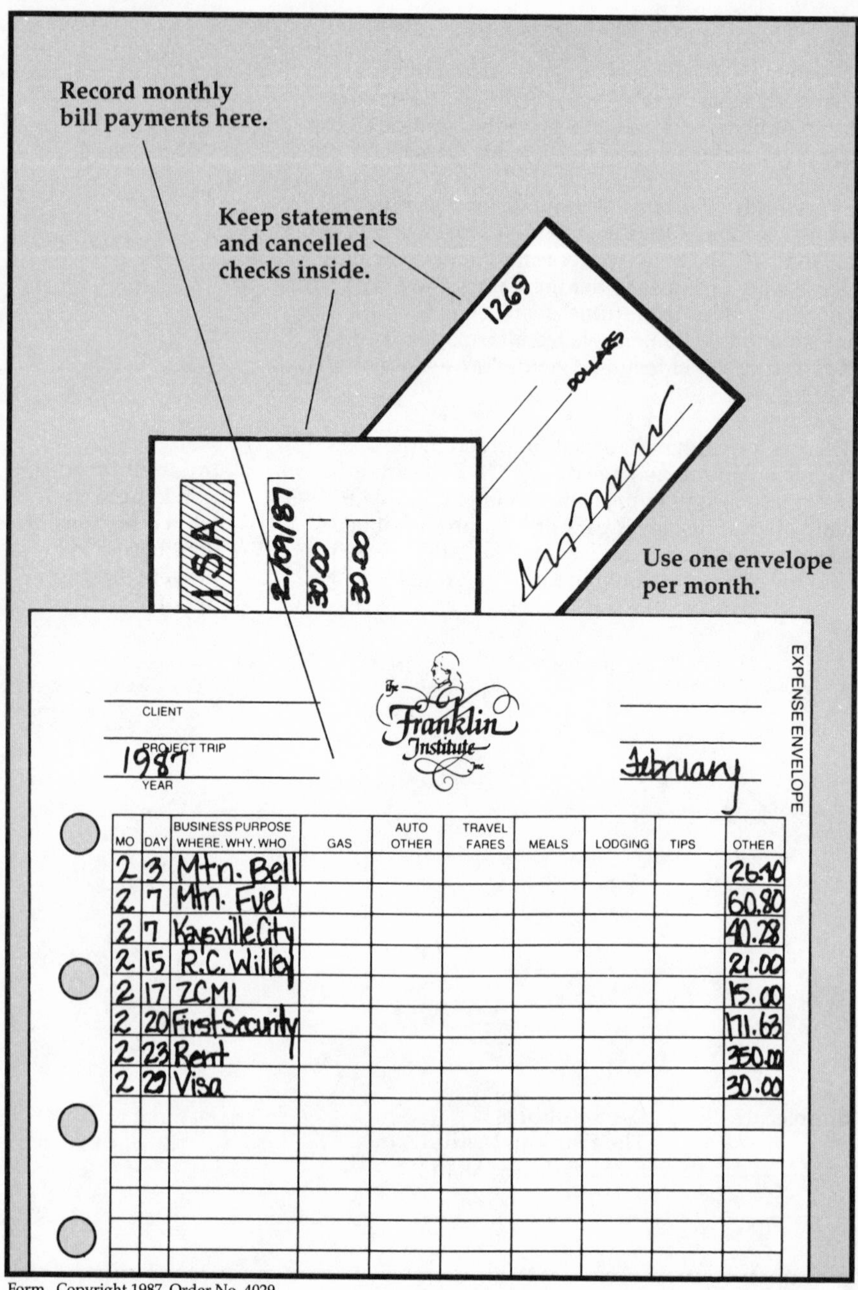

MO	DAY	BUSINESS PURPOSE WHERE, WHY, WHO	GAS	AUTO OTHER	TRAVEL FARES	MEALS	LODGING	TIPS	OTHER
2	3	Mtn. Bell							26.40
2	7	Mtn. Fuel							60.80
2	7	Kaysville City							40.28
2	15	R.C. Willey							21.00
2	17	ZCMI							15.00
2	20	First Security							171.63
2	23	Rent							350.00
2	29	Visa							30.00

Angie Cottrell had paid February's VISA bill. But in March her statement showed a previous balance due. Going back to February's records, she confirmed the check number and amount, then compared the amount paid with amount due. It took less than one minute. How did she do it? Using her Franklin Day Planner, of course.

Track your bill payments on the front of an Expense Envelope.

Angie tracks her bill payments using a monthly Expense Envelope. On the front she writes the payee, amount of payment, and payment date. Inside the envelope she keeps the statement. When her cancelled checks are returned, she includes them in the envelope also. She keeps the current month's envelope in her Planner because it is easy to find and always at her fingertips.

Because she keeps such accurate records, Angie was able to catch the discrepancy in her statement and have it corrected.

File envelopes from past months in a Storage Binder.

The Expense Envelope wasn't designed for this purpose, but . . . if the shoe fits, wear it.

Source: **Angie Cottrell**
The Franklin Institute, Inc.
Salt Lake City, Utah

Finalizing The Monthly Calendar

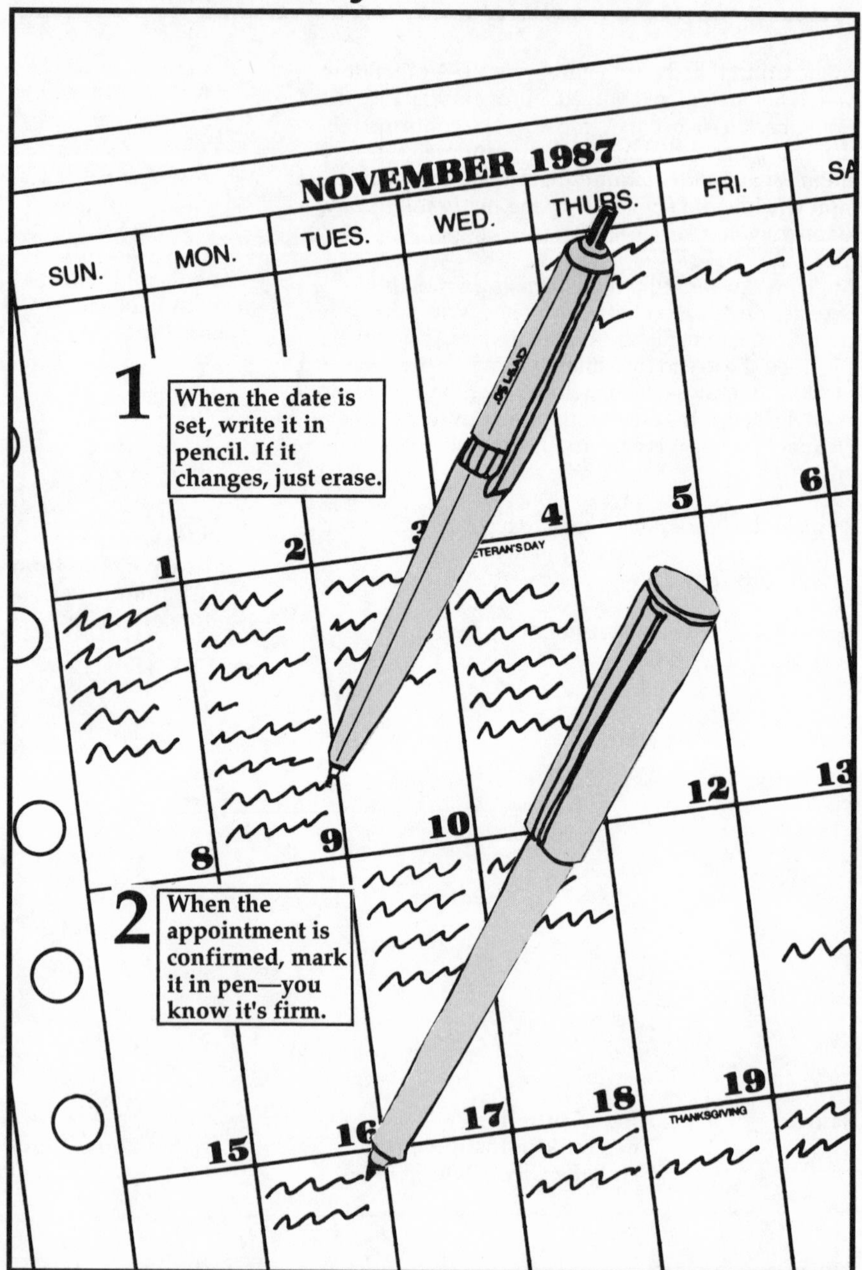

21

I was looking through Kevin Hall's Planner the other day (he is our vice president of training sales), and couldn't get over how neat it was. There was not a single word crossed out. So I asked him, "How the heck do you keep your Planner so neat? Doesn't anyone ever change meeting dates on you?" Then he explained the following:

> *At a community meeting one night, we were scheduling our monthly meetings for the next ten months or so. Everyone wrote in the dates on the Monthly Calendar of their Planner (in pen, of course). Well, about five minutes later, the chairman came in from the bathroom. We reviewed the meeting dates we had set before he had arrived and he changed every single one. We were all crossing out and rewriting meeting dates till our Planners looked like "Etch-a-Sketches." That's when I stopped writing dates in pen until they are solid. Now I note all appointments in pencil until they are confirmed. Then I write them in pen. That way, at a glance, I know whether or not I have confirmed an appointment and my Monthly Calendar is much easier to read.*

Well, I thought that was a great idea. In fact, it seems that many Day Planner users have discovered this for themselves. I'll bet Kevin's Planner would really look impressive if he could just get his kids to stop coloring in it.

Source: **Kevin Hall**
The Franklin Institute, Inc.
Salt Lake City, Utah

Solar Calculator

Order No. 4017

22

There are two controllable elements of almost everyone's life that are usually out of control—time and money. The Franklin Institute, Inc., offers Money Management seminars that teach control of economic events. Each seminar participant receives a Solar Calculator. This credit card-sized calculator runs solely on light. You don't have to turn it on or off—it works automatically according to the amount of light available. It is great for figuring a checkbook balance, comparison shopping, and doing any general math that most of us would rather do on a calculator than in our heads. It fits in the Photo Pouch and works through the plastic.

I was doing a Money Management seminar one evening at the Saginaw Club in Saginaw, Michigan. There were forty people in this big, comfortable room. When I presented the Calculator to show how it works, it didn't. There wasn't enough light anywhere in the whole building, except in the bathroom. Well, you need about 60 watts for it to work, so I don't recommend this for figuring your bill at a bar. But it's still a great little item.

Perfect for figuring; works almost anywhere.

In fact, it saved my friend Charlene Holden some headaches one day. Charlene manages our retail store. On this particular day a storm had blown down a power line. The whole company stopped. The computers, typewriters, even the phones didn't work. Neither did the cash registers. But as long as customers came to the store, Charlene sold to them. And, standing at the window, she used her trusty Solar Calculator to figure the bill. She sold a lot of calculators that day, too!

Source: **Charlene Holden**
The Franklin Institute, Inc.
Salt Lake City, Utah

Go, Call, Do

20
WEDNESDAY
MAY 20
1987

S	M	T	W	T	F	S
31					1	2
3	4	5	6	7	8	9
10	11	12	13	14	15	16
17	18	19	20	21	22	23
24	25	26	27	28	29	30

140th Day
225 Left

✓ = Task Completed
→ = Planned Forward
× = Task Deleted
G@ = Delegated Task
• = In Process

APPOINTMENT SCHEDULE

Early Morning

8

9

PRIORITIZED DAILY TASK LIST

↓	ABC PRIORITY	
✓	B2	RED-LINE MECH.
✓	B1	" ELEC.
✓	B4	" STRUC.
✓	B3	" LANDSCAPE
⊘	A	JEANNE-REVIEW W/ LEO. G.
⊙	A	L. GRASSLI - " " JEANNE
✓	A2	TIME SHEET
✓	A3	REVIEW CASH FLOW
⊘		SEE 5/18
⊘		SEE 5/18
G ✓	A1	JOHN F. GRILLE SIZE @ CENTER SPACE?
G ⊘	A	JAYELS-CANCEL DAEMS TELE?
⊘		SEE 5/14
✓		SEE 5/14
✓	A	PREPARE LIST OF ITEMS: JEANNE
✓	B6	REVIEW SPECS
→	C	SWEETS CAT. CHECK
→	C	PREPARE MISS. SUM.
⊙	A	JERRY CLARKSON-PROMO
✓	A4	PREPARE REPORT FOR RDA TONITE
→	B5	PRIORITIZE LIB/L DET.S
⊙	A	SID SMITH-50 YR. FLOOD PROT.
△		PICK UP PRINTING
△		JENNY B-DAY GIFT

DAILY EXPENSES

These symbols tell him whether the item is a GO,

- Commitments Exchanged
- Journal Entry
- Thoughts & Ideas
- Agendas (telephone, meetings)
- Conversations

MAY 1987 9:00-6:00
DAILY RECORD OF EVENTS
WEDN

LIB/L-Dave from SID SMITH's OFFICE returned
☐ He will confirm 50YR Protection req. w/ Sid.
Jeanne L. called: LIB/L
☐ ① Davis Bacon act: current wage rate needs to be in
② Adv. for bids: no info yet, but she is checking
③ asphalt pkg. will be used, concrete not allowed
④ She will prepare H.C. exclusion letter
⑤ Progress is being made on securing all property signatures-however, some are still missing. Timing
☐ ⑥ Seismic protection of stacks-she will review.
⑦ LIBRARY BUREAU Shelving: 82" & 36" avail; wood 15% + than metal shelving
☐ PREPARE DAVIS-BACON verbage to be included in s
○ called Leonard Grassli, a.m. mtg. to review w/ Jea
he will be back next Tuesday (left message)
△ ~~MARYANN-BRING SHIRT TO HER HOUSE~~
☐ BRDA-prepared progress report for RDA mtg tonite. 65% complete, 55% billed

☐ BRDA-Attended BRDA mtg and presented prog report. See notes on progress report.

OFFICE-Prepared time sheet & reviewed cash

OFFICE 1.5
LIB/L 4.5
BRDA 2.5+1.0+1.5

or a CALL

or a DO

23

Doug Todd wrote that he is a "believer" since using the Franklin Planner, but the Planner lacked one element vital for him—phone, task, and errand categories.

So he made up his own symbols for the Prioritized Daily Task List to indicate this:

△ Outside Office—Go

○ Telephone—Call

□ Task—Do

He also uses these symbols on the Daily Record of Events page as a reminder of things that need to be done but have not yet been scheduled.

Source: **Douglas Todd**
Todd Associates, Architects
Bountiful, Utah

Balancing The Franklin Day Planner

If you find it difficult to write in the Planner because of the rings, put the Colored Tab sections at the front of the Planner.

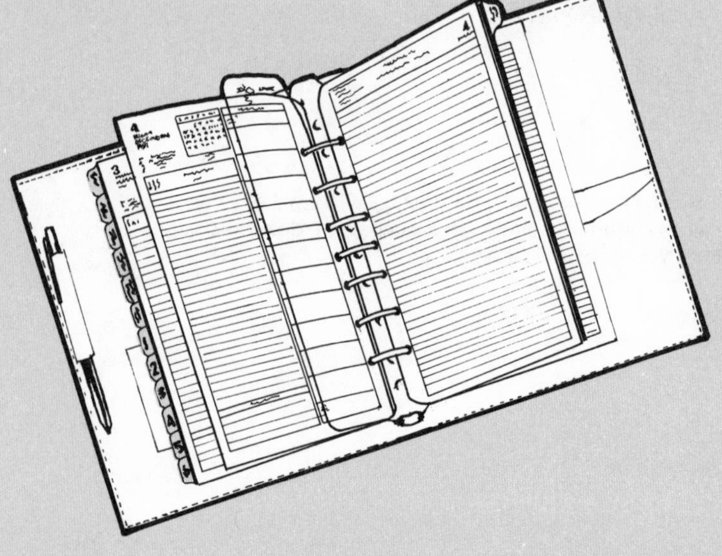

"Rebalancing" the Planner makes the pages lie at the same level as the rings—the rings don't interfere with writing in the book.

Sometimes people tell me the Franklin Day Planner is off balance. When open to the daily page, more pages lie on the right side of the Planner than on the other side. When writing, particularly in the Appointment section, the rings get in the way.

Mary Detmar and her friends at the Idaho Transportation Department have rearranged their Planners with the daily pages behind (rather than in front of) the Colored Tabs, making it easier to write in the Appointment Schedule. This also helps left-handed writers.

Kevin Hall, when he encounters this question, now recommends to his seminar participants that they "re-balance" the Planner, using the same technique that Mary discovered.

Source: **Mary Detmar**
Idaho Transportation Department
Boise, Idaho

Daily Mileage Records

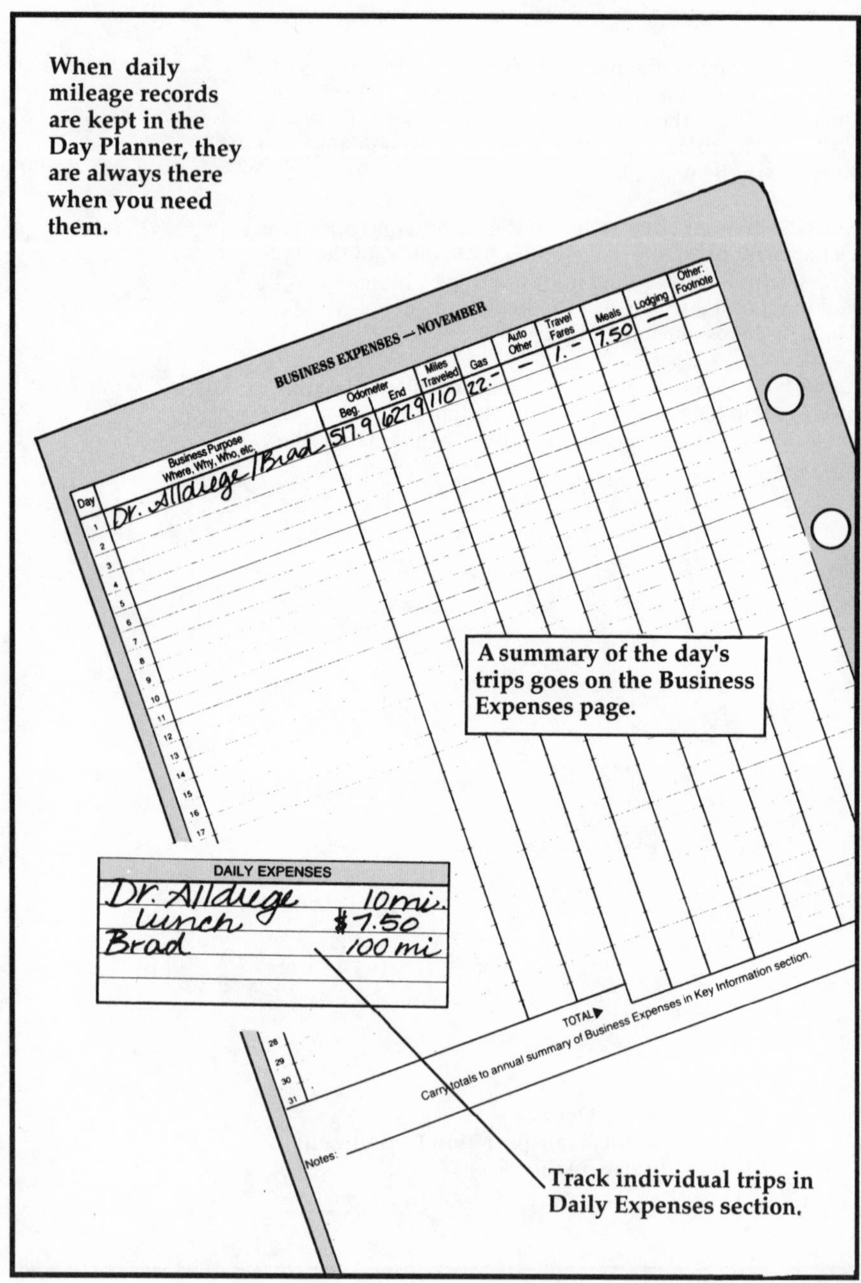

When daily mileage records are kept in the Day Planner, they are always there when you need them.
BUSINESS EXPENSES — NOVEMBER
Day
Business Purpose Where, Why, Who, etc.
Odometer
Beg.
End
Miles Traveled
Gas
Auto Other
Travel Fares
Meals
Lodging
Other: Footnote
Dr. Alldiege / Brad
517.9
627.9
110
22.-
1.-
7.50
A summary of the day's trips goes on the Business Expenses page.
DAILY EXPENSES
Dr. Alldiege 10 mi.
lunch $7.50
Brad 100 mi
TOTAL▶
Carry totals to annual summary of Business Expenses in Key Information section.
Notes:
Track individual trips in Daily Expenses section.

Keeping track of mileage, whether for yourself, the accountant, or the IRS, can be a real hassle. Company forms usually drift between the passenger seat, the glove box, and the floor of your car. When there is no form, mileage figures end up on floating pieces of paper that overtake your glove box. If you keep a little notebook in your car, that's where it is when the accountant wants the information—in your car. Your Day Planner is the perfect place to keep track of mileage; it's always with you and it doesn't float.

Avoid recording mileage on papers or forms that "float."

The last page of each month, entitled Business Expenses, is for recording mileage. It works best if you record only one trip per day. If you must record several trips per day, you may need more room. Try recording mileage in the Daily Expenses space of the daily page, then summarizing the day's trips on the Business Expenses page. Or use a Blank Lined Paper behind a Red Tab set aside for business expenses. This allows space for more detail, such as purpose of the trip, whom you are visiting, etc. (You may also choose to keep an Expense Envelope behind this tab to record other business expenses.) If you need to use a company form, most can be seven-hole punched to keep in the Planner.

All yearly records, then, are kept in a Storage Binder for tax purposes. Next March, your accountant will thank me for this.

The Order of the Book

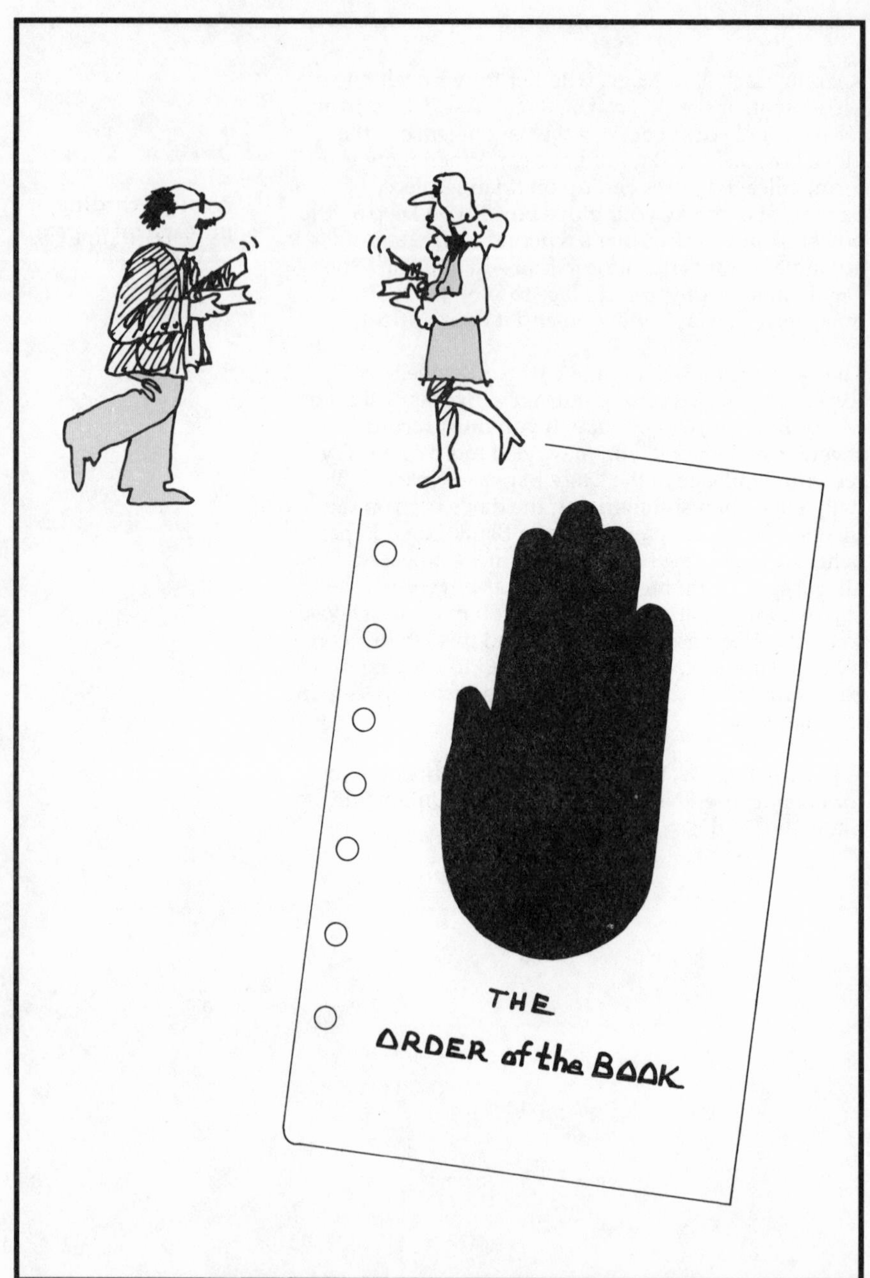

26

In the Time Management seminar, I tell of Dow Chemical's "Order of the Book." When two employees with Franklin Day Planners pass in the halls they do a special wave that signifies they are members of the "Order of the Book:" holding the Planner flat in one hand, they flash open the top cover with the other hand.

Tom Young has drawn a logo for the "Order of the Book." When he sees strangers with a Franklin Day Planner in the elevator or on the street, he flashes his logo at them, and they both get a chuckle.

What *have* we started here?!

Sources: **Dow Chemical Employees**
Midland, Michigan

Tom Young
Young Electric Sign Company
Salt Lake City, Utah

The Peek-Ahead Approach

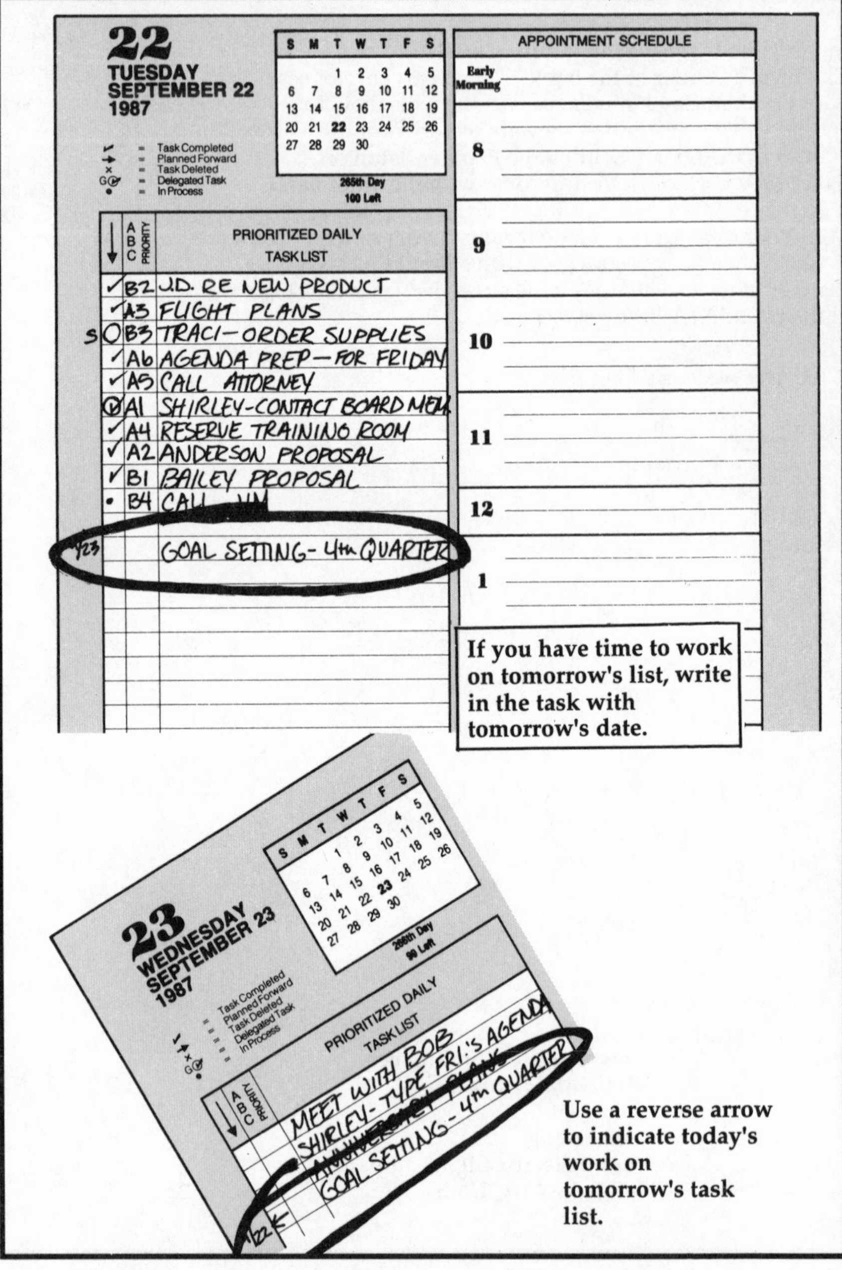

If you have time to work on tomorrow's list, write in the task with tomorrow's date.

Use a reverse arrow to indicate today's work on tomorrow's task list.

27

Stewart Morick has a problem that few people have ever experienced, but would probably love to. He gets all his daily tasks done early—there's still day left at the end of his list. He attributes this to effective use of his Franklin Planner. He describes how he deals with this problem:

> *When all today's tasks are complete, delegated, and/or in process, I turn to tomorrow's task list (I call this the "peek-ahead" approach). From this list I choose one item to work on now. I generally choose a "fun" rather than a "have to" task.*
>
> *On tomorrow's list, I place a reverse arrow and today's date. This way, I can refer back to it when I do tomorrow's planning.*
>
> *On today's list I enter the task with tomorrow's date. If I complete the task, I check it off in today's column. If I do not complete the task, I place a forward arrow in the symbols column telling me to continue working on it tomorrow (where it is already on the Daily Task List).*
>
> *Tomorrow, during my daily planning session, the reverse arrow and date instruct me to go backwards. I review the status of the task. Then I check it as already completed or I prioritize it for completion. In most cases, I have already begun the task and it's only a matter of completing it.*
>
> *This helps in two ways: (1) I keep ahead which frees up valuable time for future tasks—I call this "banking time"—and (2) I have time to do enjoyable things.*

As you keep ahead, you can "bank" your time!

That sounds like a great idea—no one ever said you have to wait until tomorrow just because the task is on tomorrow's list!

Source: **Stewart Morick**
Price Waterhouse
Washington, D.C.

The Quick Clip

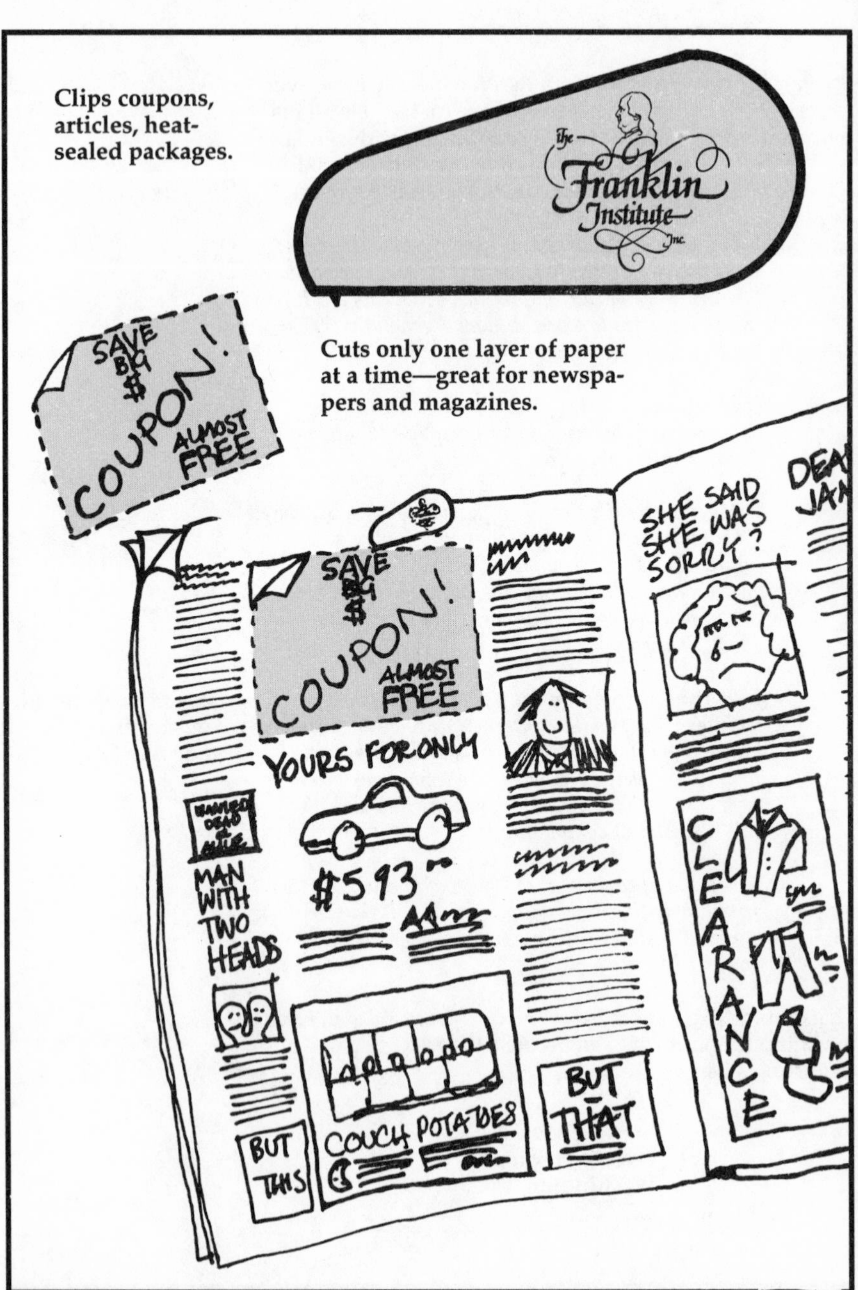

Order No. 4018

This is another little novelty for saving time and space and making you more efficient. It's called a Quick Clip, because it clips things quick! It's rather unassuming, and looks like an oversized guitar pick. But place the flat edge on paper, draw it towards you, and it cuts just the top layer. It works great for clipping newspaper or magazine articles, coupons, and even for opening heat-sealed packages (like the ones the Planner refills come in). It's small enough to keep in a Zipper Pouch, or in the business card pocket of a binder, so it's always with you.

Clips coupons, articles, heat-sealed packages.

Now when you see an article you would like to read, you can clip it out and seven-hole punch it for your Planner. The next time you are waiting at an appointment, or have three minutes to spare, the article is with you!

Reduce and punch articles and keep them in your Planner to read while waiting for appointments.

Source: **Glen Davis**
Bountiful, Utah

Phone Section

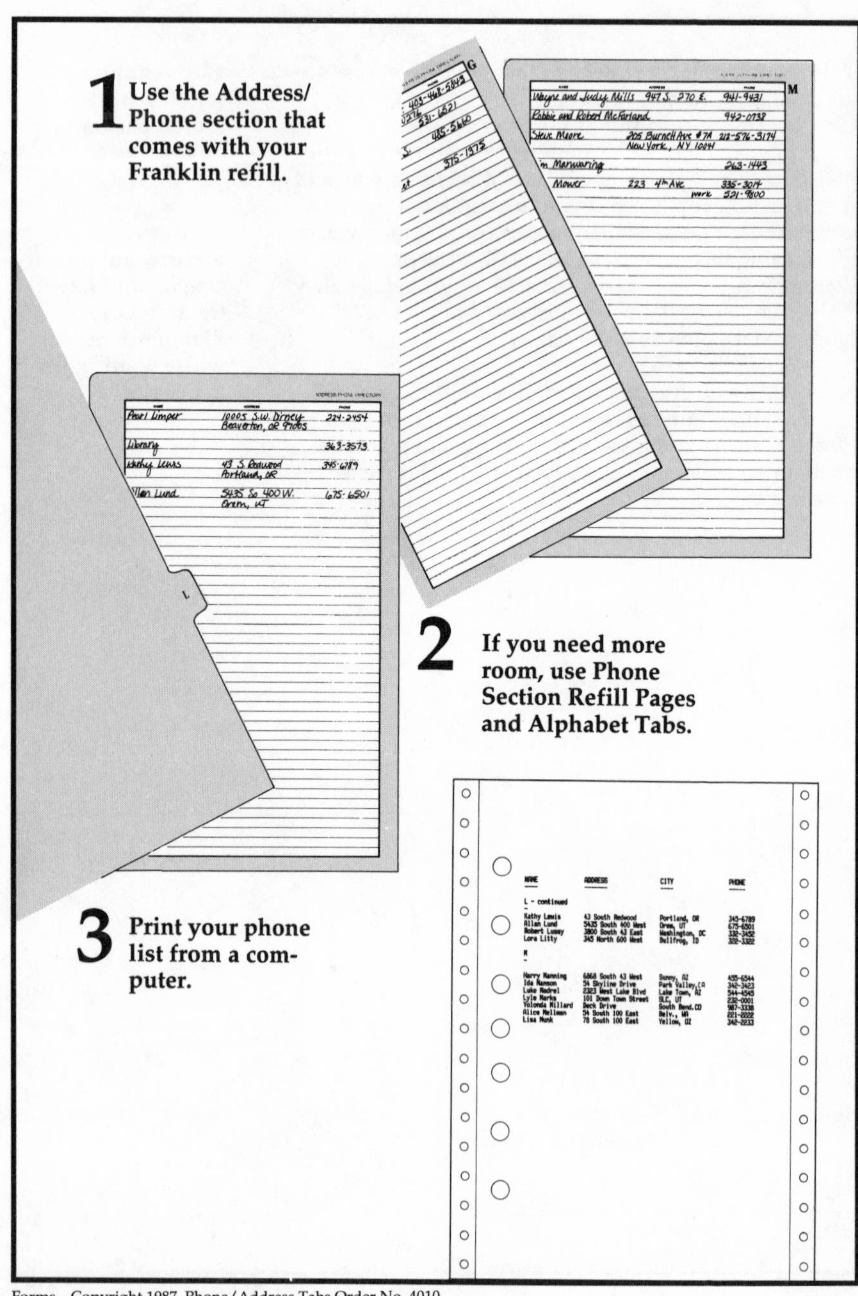

1 Use the Address/ Phone section that comes with your Franklin refill.
2 If you need more room, use Phone Section Refill Pages and Alphabet Tabs.
3 Print your phone list from a computer.

Forms Copyright 1987 Phone/Address Tabs Order No. 4010
Alphabet Tabs Order No. 4043

Keeping frequently used phone numbers nearby is vital to maintaining a high level of productivity. The Address/Phone section included in your Planner allows for one page per letter, or about fourteen complete names and addresses. Many people need more room than that. There are various solutions to this problem.

The Address/Phone section of your Day Planner can be adapted to your own specific needs.

The phone section is available tabbed, with two letters per tab. New Phone Section Refill Pages are available to allow for two or more pages for each letter of the phone section. Alphabet Tabs are also available with one letter per tab. These are generic—insert the Phone Section Refill Pages to allow for many pages per letter.

Tom Young prints out his phone section from a personal computer and reduces and punches it for the Planner. (The Institute also sells Continuous Form Computer Paper in Day Planner size; see idea 13.) A computerized list can be as extensive as you like; it is easy to update and saves space in the Planner.

Source: **Tom Young**
Young Electric Sign Co.
Salt Lake City, Utah

Multiple Pen Holder

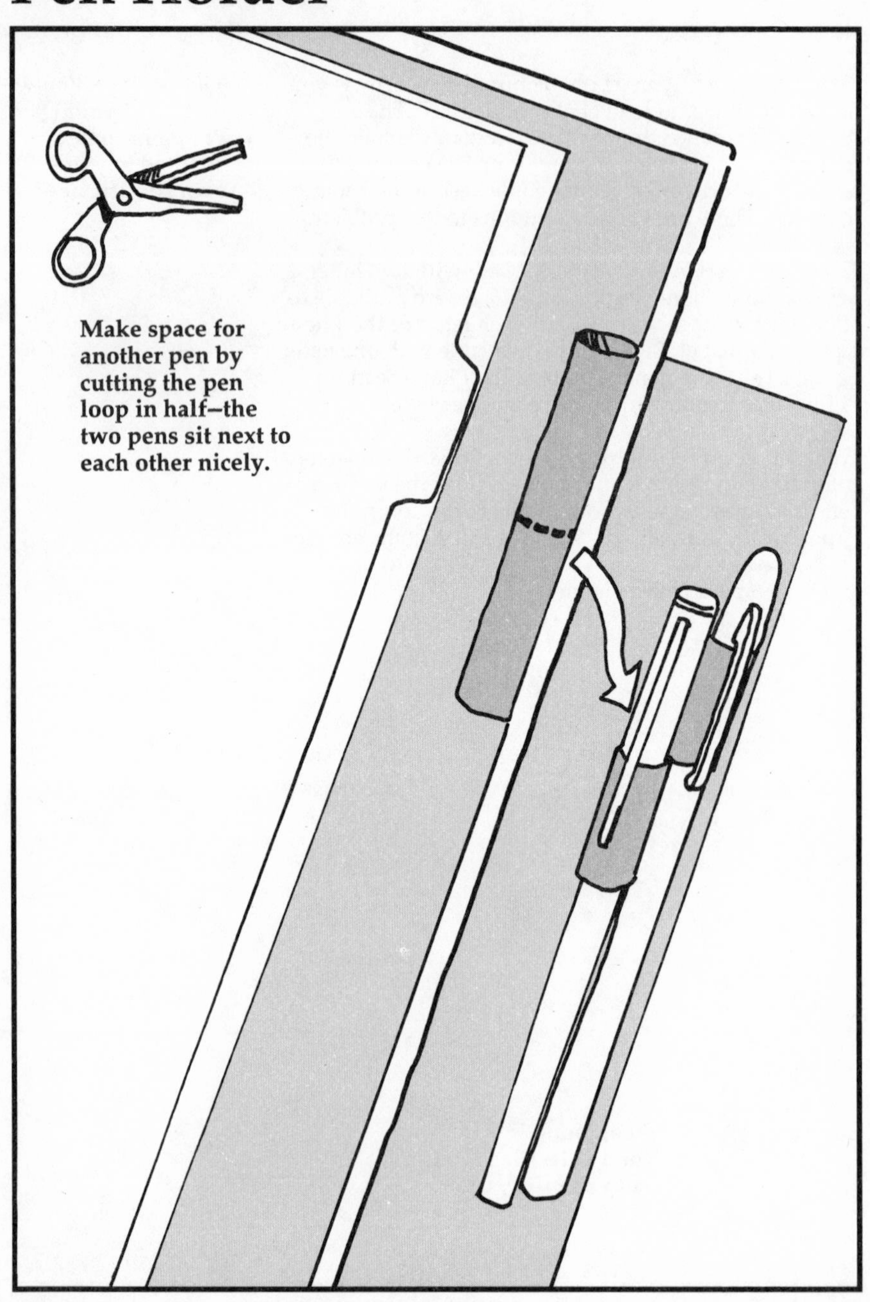

Make space for another pen by cutting the pen loop in half—the two pens sit next to each other nicely.

Greg Fullerton needed more than one pen in his binder. But he had bought his leather binder before we began making them with two pen loops instead of one.

So Greg solved the problem for himself. With a razor blade, he cut the pen loop in half, making two loops. One pen sits to the right, and one to the left.

Make your own pen pocket to hold three extra implements. Set on the edge of the binder, it won't interfere with the pages when the book is closed.

Milton Schaefer has a small plastic pocket glued onto the inside front cover of his binder, very close to the outside edge, to keep two or three pens or pencils. It is small enough that the book closes without interference.

Now that you can keep more colors and types of pens or pencils in your binder, you may want to refer to idea 3 to learn what to do with them.

Sources: **Greg Fullerton**
The Franklin Institute, Inc.
Salt Lake City, Utah

Milton E. Schaefer
Los Angeles, California

Project Management

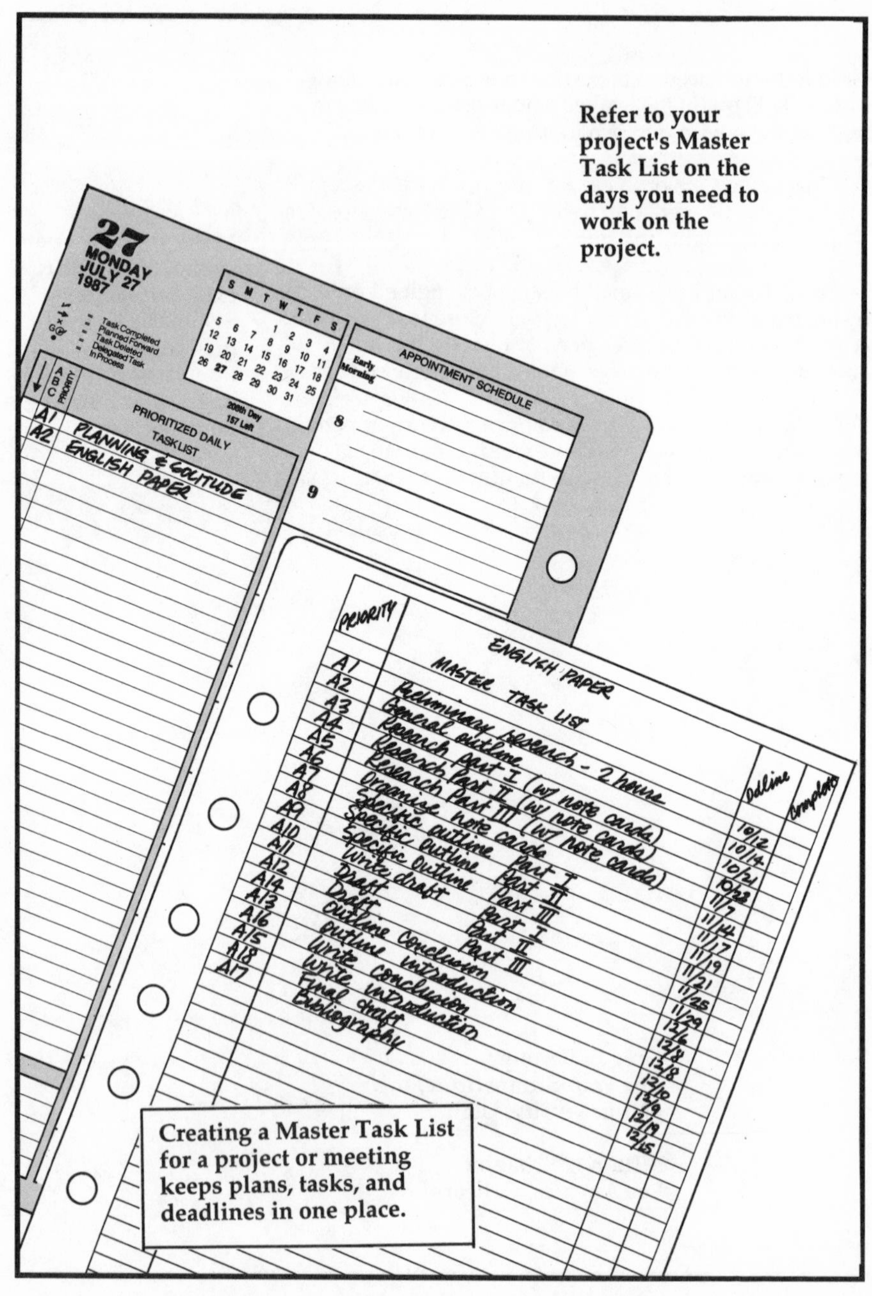

Refer to your project's Master Task List on the days you need to work on the project.

Creating a Master Task List for a project or meeting keeps plans, tasks, and deadlines in one place.

31

Few major projects can be accomplished at one sitting, or even in one day. Whether preparing a report or doing spring cleaning, several tasks are planned over a period of many days to get the job done. When working with a deadline, it is especially helpful to map out the project at the onset using the Day Planner.

When Eugene Fischer schedules an appointment or meeting that requires a lot of preparation, he immediately plugs in mini-deadlines to complete the preparations. He paces himself, thus avoiding last-minute late nights, and allows time for those emergencies that always seem to crop up.

My daughter has had some wonderful experiences with this idea. At the beginning of the term last year, her English teacher assigned a term paper to be due the last week of class. That night I sat down with her to map it out. We started with an outline of all tasks required to successfully complete the paper with an A grade. We identified time frames, elements, and people, then prioritized and numbered them. This outline became the Master Task List for the project. Then we scheduled in each task on her Daily Task Lists, making reference to the Master Task List.

One week later, my daughter found in her Daily Task List the first reference to the project. Turning to the project's Master List, she began with task A1, two hours of preliminary research.

She finished the term paper four days early. Have you ever finished anything four days early? The teacher was amazed and her classmates intimidated. Boy, I wish I'd had one of these Planners in high school!

Sources:

Eugene M. Fischer
Swenson Anderson Associates
Minneapolis, Minnesota

Stacie Smith
Viewmont High School
Centerville, Utah

Blocking Appointment Times:
DOTS AND LINES

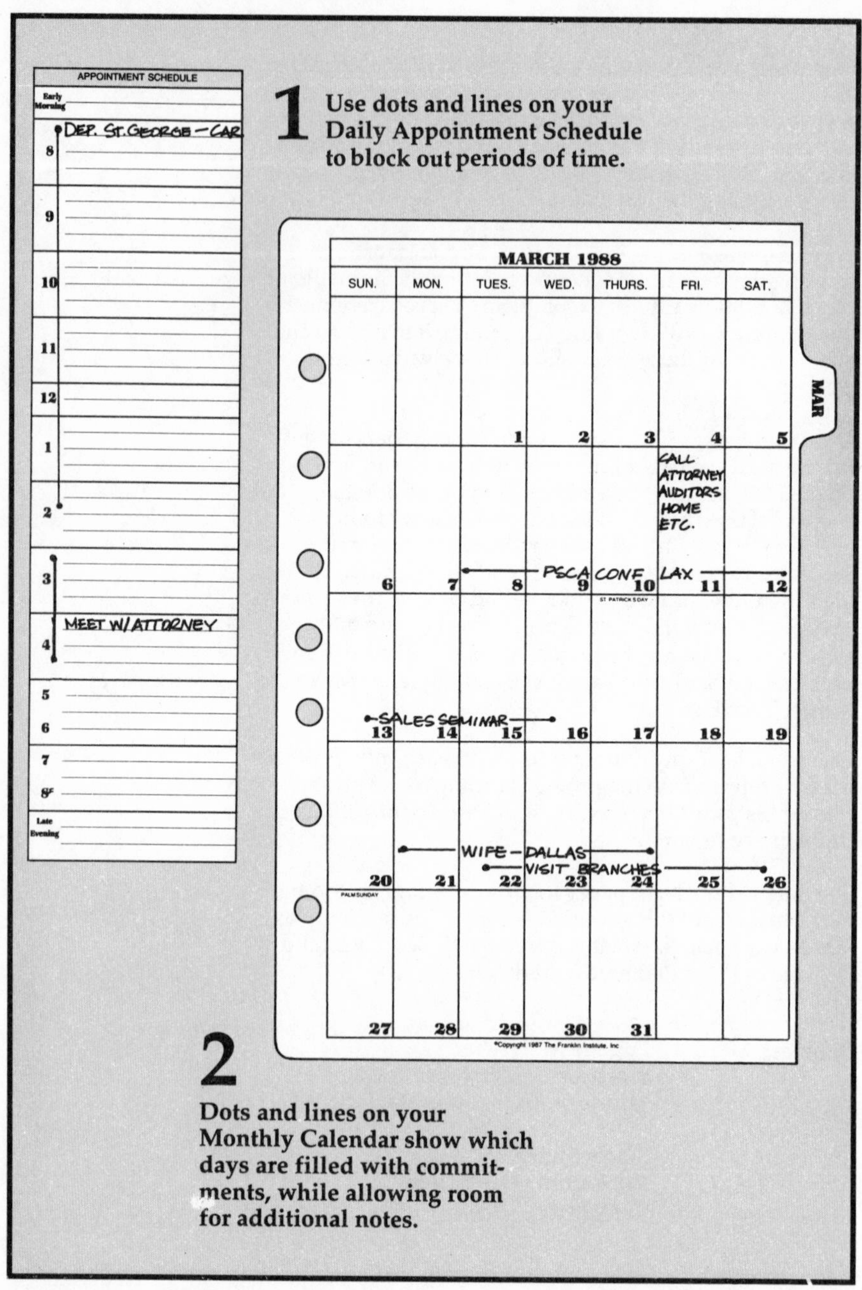

APPOINTMENT SCHEDULE
Early Morning
DEP. ST. GEORGE—CAR
MEET W/ ATTORNEY
Late Evening
1 Use dots and lines on your Daily Appointment Schedule to block out periods of time.
MARCH 1988
SUN. MON. TUES. WED. THURS. FRI. SAT.
MAR
CALL ATTORNEY AUDITORS HOME ETC.
PSCA CONF LAX
ST. PATRICK'S DAY
SALES SEMINAR
WIFE—DALLAS
VISIT BRANCHES
PALM SUNDAY
©Copyright 1987 The Franklin Institute, Inc
2 Dots and lines on your Monthly Calendar show which days are filled with commitments, while allowing room for additional notes.

32

Tom Young was tired of writing in the exact times of his appointments on the daily Appointment Schedule. So he devised a dot and line system to block out times.

If an appointment begins at 3:00 p.m., he places a dot to the left of the first space in the box labeled 3:00. If it ends at 4:45 p.m., he places another dot to the left of the third space in the 4:00 box. Then he draws a line between the two dots. This visually indicates to him what time the meeting will begin and end, and blocks out the time in between, preventing him from over-scheduling.

He employs the same system on the Monthly Calendar, this time using horizontal (across days) rather than vertical lines. On the Monthly Calendar, he uses dots and lines for major events, such as trips and conventions, rather than daily meetings. Above the horizontal lines, there is space to record other obligations. If he leaves midday, the dot is placed in the middle of the daily space (horizontally), and if he returns late evening, the line extends to the far right of the daily space, visually "blocking out" that day.

Source: **Tom Young**
Young Electric Sign Company
Salt Lake City, Utah

Yearly Events Reminder

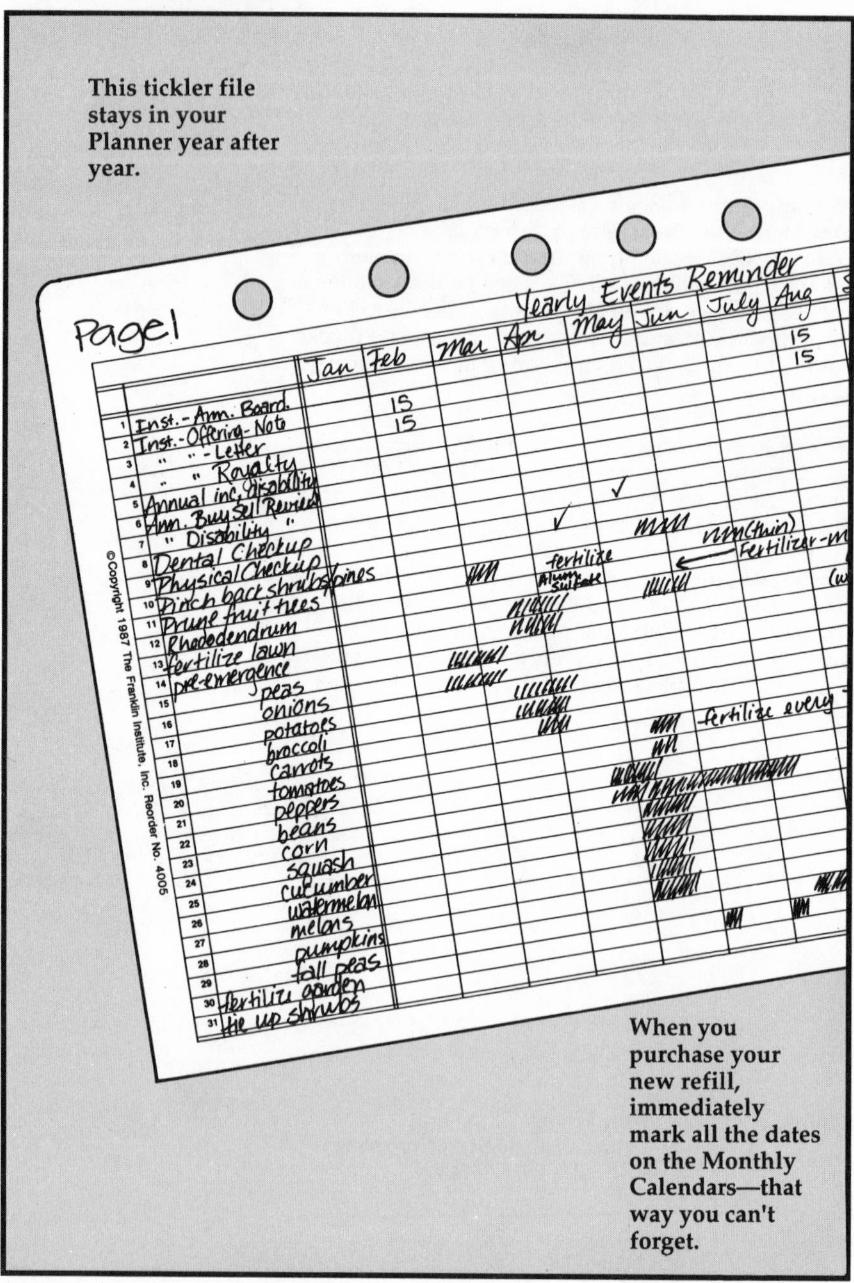

This tickler file stays in your Planner year after year.

When you purchase your new refill, immediately mark all the dates on the Monthly Calendars—that way you can't forget.

33

Have you ever missed a yearly deadline or renewal date or even a birthday? Those once-a-year activities are frequently forgotten or procrastinated, and that kind of mistake almost always costs money.

Lynn Robbins, senior vice president at Franklin, makes a Yearly Events Reminder from a 13 Column Spread Sheet. The twelve months go in the columns, and the events on the thirty-one lines. He keeps this page in the Planning Calendar section, and plugs the dates into hisMonthly Calendars at each new year.

He keeps all kinds of information on this sheet: birthdays and anniversaries, reminders for medical and dental checkups, and annual meetings such as stockholders or board meetings. Yearly events may also include loan maturity dates and lease renewals, maintenance on major appliances (such as air conditioner and furnace), or auto safety inspections and emissions tests.

Add new items to this list as they are established—so you won't forget next year.

Renewal dates also go on this reminder list: auto license, business or real estate license, insurance policies, memberships, and magazine subscriptions.

You can tickle your memory for any annual, semi-annual, or quarterly event using this simple reminder.

Source: **Lynn G. Robbins**
The Franklin Institute, Inc.
Salt Lake City, Utah

An Alarm Clock For Your Binder

Set the alarm for appointments so you don't forget to notice the time!

It was Kathleen's first day at the Franklin Institute. Jean, her new boss, had shown her the ropes and put her to work on some paste-up projects. About 2:30, Kathleen heard a "beep-beep-beep-beep." She thought maybe this was a subtle reminder for break time so she left her desk to get a soda. No one was in the lunch room, so she returned to her desk. She went in to ask Jean what it was, but Jean wasn't there. The next day, she heard it again, this time at 11:00 a.m. and again at 3:30 p.m. *The break schedules around here sure are strange*, she thought. After a week of this, she finally asked Jean why the break bell rang at different times every day. When Jean figured out what Kathleen was talking about, she explained her binder alarm clock:

A small round digital clock will fit easily on the inside edge of your binder.

Jean gets very involved in her projects—so much so that she used to forget appointments. Writing in her Day Planner only helped when she remembered to look in the Planner! So she bought a little round auto clock with an alarm. The clock is stuck to the inside of her binder. Every morning, she sets the alarm for any meeting or appointment she may have that day.

Others around her get a chuckle every time the alarm goes off, but Jean doesn't miss appointments anymore. I think for Christmas I'll get her one of those alarms that plays classical tunes.

Source: **Jean Canestrini**
The Franklin Institute, Inc.
Salt Lake City, Utah

More on Mileage

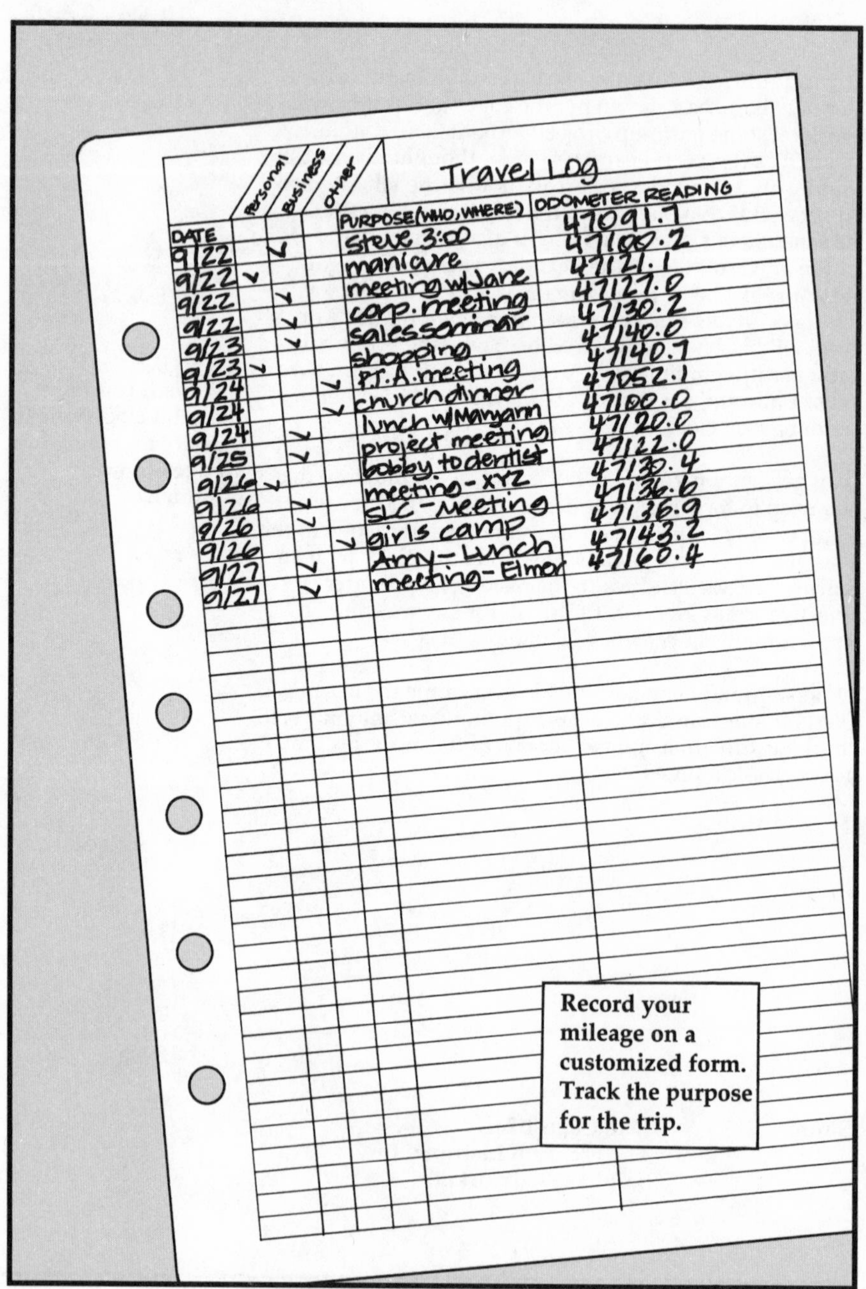

Travel Log

DATE	Personal	Business	Other	PURPOSE (WHO, WHERE)	ODOMETER READING
9/22		✓		Steve 3:00	47091.7
9/22	✓			manicure	47100.2
9/22		✓		meeting w/Jane	47121.1
9/22		✓		corp. meeting	47127.0
9/23		✓		sales seminar	47130.2
9/23	✓			shopping	47140.0
9/24			✓	P.T.A. meeting	47140.7
9/24			✓	church dinner	47052.1
9/24		✓		lunch w/Maryann	47100.0
9/25		✓		project meeting	47120.0
9/26	✓			bobby to dentist	47122.0
9/26		✓		meeting-XYZ	47130.4
9/26		✓		SLC-Meeting	47136.6
9/26			✓	girls camp	47136.9
9/27		✓		Amy-Lunch	47143.2
9/27		✓		meeting-Elmor	47160.4

Record your mileage on a customized form. Track the purpose for the trip.

In idea 25 I mentioned several ways to record mileage in the Franklin Planner. Just last week I received a letter from Bonnie McCullough with a copy of her customized mileage form.

Bonnie has a company car, but also uses it for personal and church errands. To track it all, she has made her own form.

Every time she pulls into the driveway, she records the trip on this form. After dating the first column, she checks whether the trip was for business, church, or personal use. The next column includes where she went and/or whom she visited. In the last column she writes the ending odometer reading. (She writes only the end because every trip is recorded, so the last entry is the beginning reading for the next trip.)

At the end of the year, all mileage information is together and easily figured for taxes.

Her husband also keeps a sheet in his car. Together at the end of each month, they tally the categories.

They keep the forms on a clipboard in the car, then store full sheets in the year's Storage Binder. At the end of the year, all mileage information is together and easily figured for taxes. Bonnie said that keeping track of mileage has saved their family hundreds of dollars in taxes.

Source: **Bonnie McCullough**
Lakewood, Colorado

Family Information

Customize your own Personal Information section to include any details you wish to remember.

Page 2

[F]AMILY INFORMATION

[B]irthday: 12/17/74 Bloodtype: O+

[...]1234 Driver's License: Not yet!

Neck: 14 Waist: 30

Sleeve Length: 30 Inseam: 36

Sweater: Med. Coat Size: 32

Shoe Size: 10½

PREFERENCES:

Favorite Color: Blue Cologne: —

Music: Elvis Costello, Thompson Twins Latest Fad: Soccer

Friends/Phone Numbers: Jack 555-6374

Darryl 555-7119

Johnny 555-5263

Teacher's Name: Mrs. Stuart

Name: Jill Birthday: 1/25/71 Bloodtype: A+

S.S.#: 528-00-4321 Driver's License: 147611567

CLOTHING SIZES:

Dress: 8 Pants: 8

Blouse: 8 Sweater: Med.

Skirt: 8 Shoe Size: 7½

PREFERENCES:

Favorite Color: Red Cologne: Gloria Vanderbilt

Music: Alabama, The Judds Latest Fad: Teddy bears

Friends/Phone Numbers: Janice 555-1634

Lisa 555-6431

Ryan 555-1123

Traci 555-4737

Teachers: Eng: Mr. Johnson. Math: Miss Simmons

36

My wife and I have a dear friend, Georgianna Bixford, who has eight children ranging in age from eighteen months to eighteen years. She is hard-pressed to keep track of clothing sizes, blood types, vaccinations and health records, and favorite rock and roll bands for each of her children.

Expand your Key Information section to make details about your family more accessible.

Gail (my wife) showed her the Key Information section in the Franklin Planner, and Georgianna got excited. But there simply is not enough room on the Personal Information page for all the vital data she wanted on each family member (not to mention extended family). Not one to be overcome by circumstance, Georgianna made her own Personal Information section for her Planner.

Now she has every little detail, right down to the latest greatest fad, on all her children. She said that shopping for birthdays has never been so easy!

Source: **Georgianna Bixford**
Mobile, Alabama

Correcting The Monthly Calendar

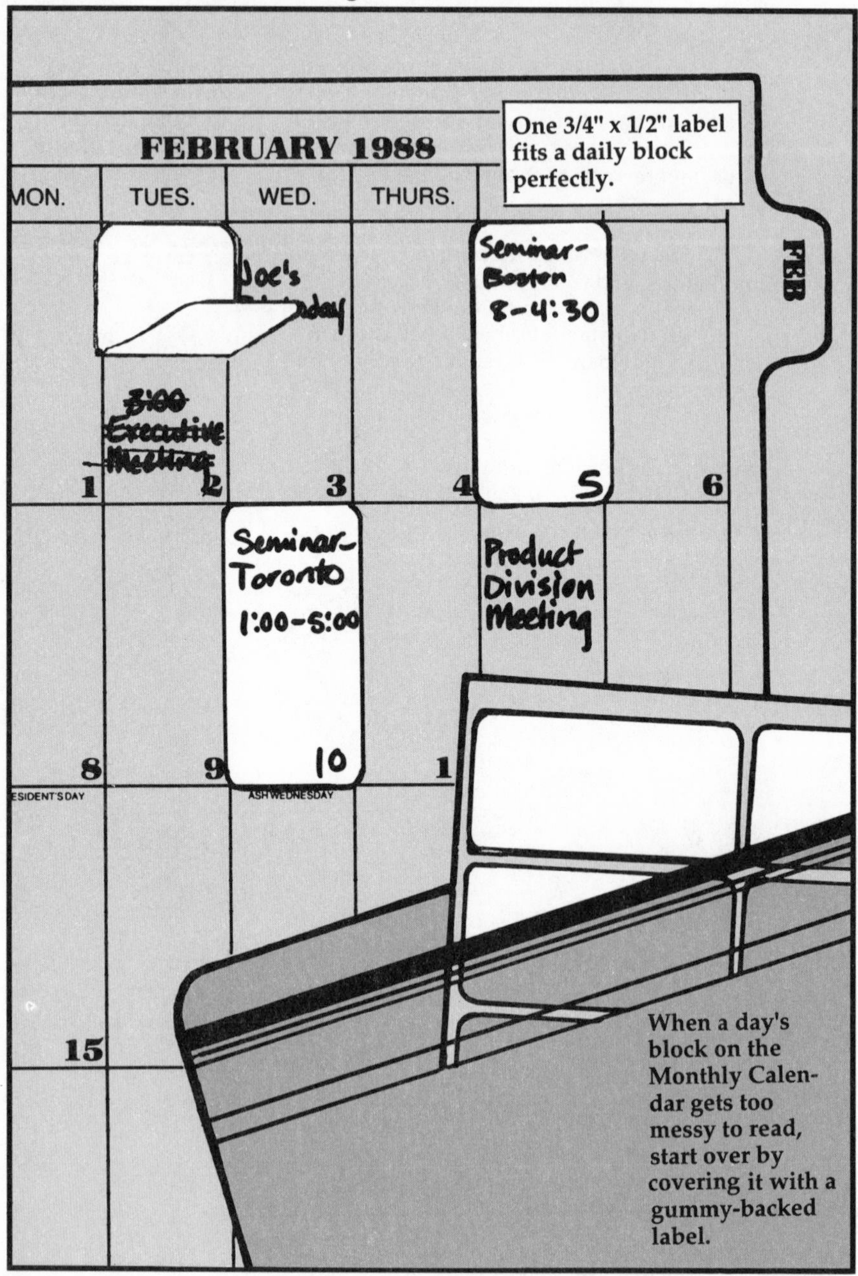

One 3/4" x 1/2" label fits a daily block perfectly.

When a day's block on the Monthly Calendar gets too messy to read, start over by covering it with a gummy-backed label.

37

In the Franklin Store, people often ask for extra Monthly Tabs. The most common reason is they "botched" it—wrote and later changed things so much that they finally wanted to throw out their Monthly Tab and start over. Instead of going through extra Monthly Calendars, we have come up with some other ideas to solve this problem. Ideas 21 and 70 offer some very good suggestions. Here is another:

Dennis Webb regularly keeps gummy-backed Avery labels (3/4" x 1 1/2") in his Zipper Pouch. These fit perfectly over the daily space on the Monthly Calendar. When a particular day becomes hopelessly unreadable, he simply covers it with a white label and starts over.

Source: **Dennis Webb**
The Franklin Institute, Inc.
Salt Lake City, Utah

Waiting Projects

"Waiting projects" reduce the tension of unexpected waits.

"It's heavy traffic on this Friday afternoon. We've got a three-car collision blocking two lanes on I-15 and traffic is backed up for miles. Avoid the freeway at all costs. This is Bill Freeway reporting—have a great weekend!!"

And Belinda Meldrum was right in the middle of it all. Traffic was at a standstill. But instead of swearing, she balanced her checkbook and planned the agenda for a meeting. She got home an hour late that night but didn't mind—she had gotten more done than ever possible had she been at home!

She has learned one of the values of having the Planner with her all the time: making good use of unexpected free moments.

Keep mail, bills, and articles in the binder. Work on them when you have a spare moment.

Janice Kimberlin finds herself waiting a lot: in the doctor's office, at a restaurant, at school waiting for the professor to show up, or in long lines. She stashes mail, reading material, and bills in the pockets of her binder, so she can use the time to get a few things done.

Belinda calls these tasks "waiting projects." They have reduced tension and stress in waiting situations so much that she feels cheated now when she doesn't have to wait for the doctor!

Sources:

Belinda Meldrum
Salt Lake City, Utah

Janice Kimberlin
Englehard Corporation
Iselin, New Jersey

In Case of Loss or Theft

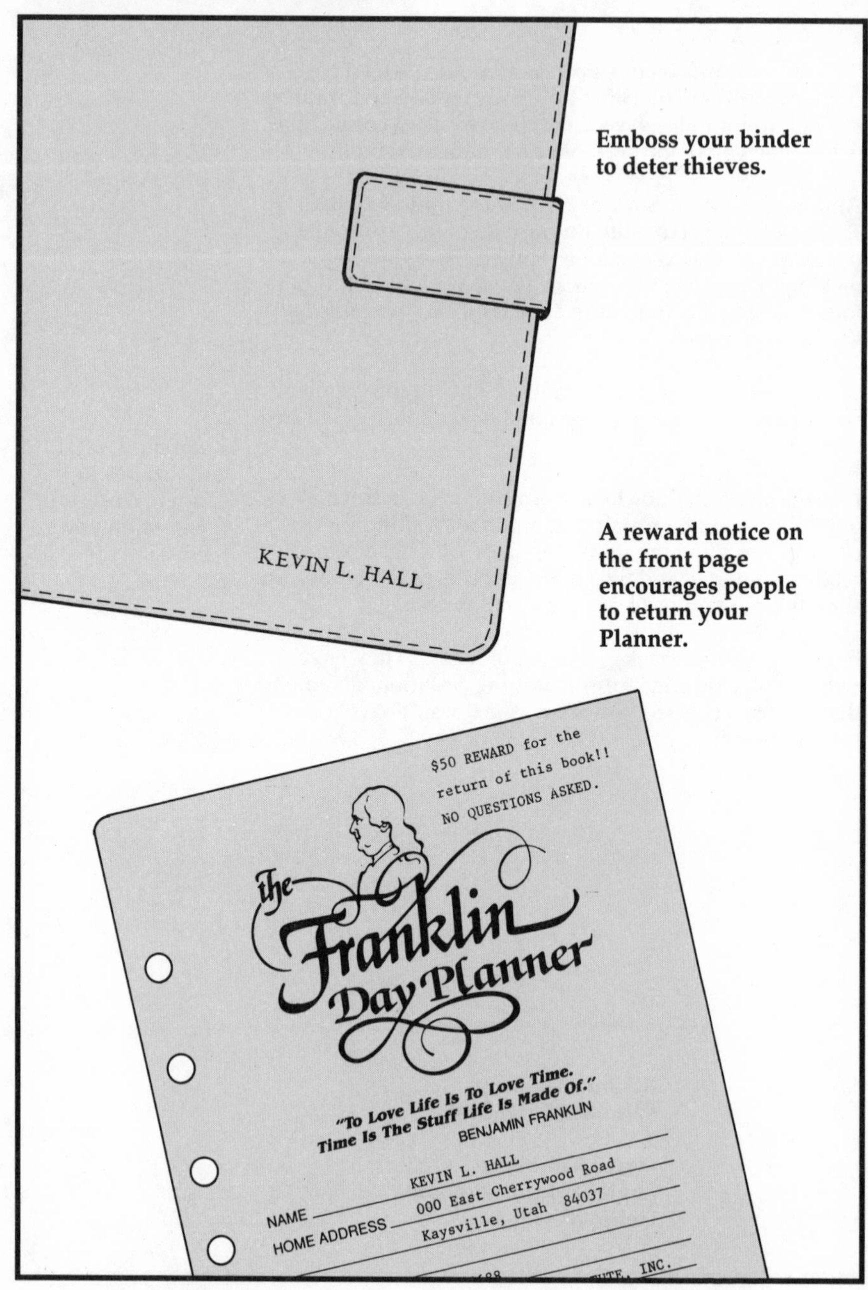

Emboss your binder to deter thieves.
KEVIN L. HALL
A reward notice on the front page encourages people to return your Planner.
$50 REWARD for the return of this book!! NO QUESTIONS ASKED.
The Franklin Day Planner
"To Love Life Is To Love Time. Time Is The Stuff Life Is Made Of."
BENJAMIN FRANKLIN
NAME
KEVIN L. HALL
HOME ADDRESS
000 East Cherrywood Road
Kaysville, Utah 84037

39

It's frightening to think what would happen if I lost my Planner. People tell me things like, "I'd die without my Franklin!" or "I'd be helpless without it," or "I can't remember how I managed before I had my Planner."

While loss or theft is rare, it happens. A few simple precautions can make all the difference in your ability to cope if yours disappears.

Kevin Hall keeps a notice on the front page of his Planner: "$50 REWARD for the return of this book!! NO QUESTIONS ASKED." For fifty dollars, a thief may reconsider, and you can bet that any finder will call Kevin within the day.

Copy all important information and keep it at home. That way you only lose the convenience—not the information.

If the Planner isn't returned, however, frustration and helplessness may set in. Your Planner contains all kinds of information that is found nowhere else! Beth Hottinger is very concerned about losing her Planner. She makes copies of all important information and stores them at home. She says, "If something happens to the Planner, I will only lose the convenience of having the information at my fingertips, not the information itself."

Jeanine Ogilvy keeps spare keys in her Planner, and therefore recommends writing only a business address in the Planner, never the home address. Should the Planner be stolen, the stranger cannot use the keys.

If someone is tempted to take your beautiful leather binder, your name embossed on the front may make it less appealing.

Keep it with you!

But the best way to prevent loss is to carry it with you! One gentleman said he always notices immediately when his Planner is missing because his left arm feels light!

Sources:

Beth Hottinger
Dow Chemical
Midland, Michigan

Jeanine Ogilvy
New York, New York

Kevin L. Hall
The Franklin Institute, Inc.
Salt Lake City, Utah

The Wallet and The Franklin Day Planner

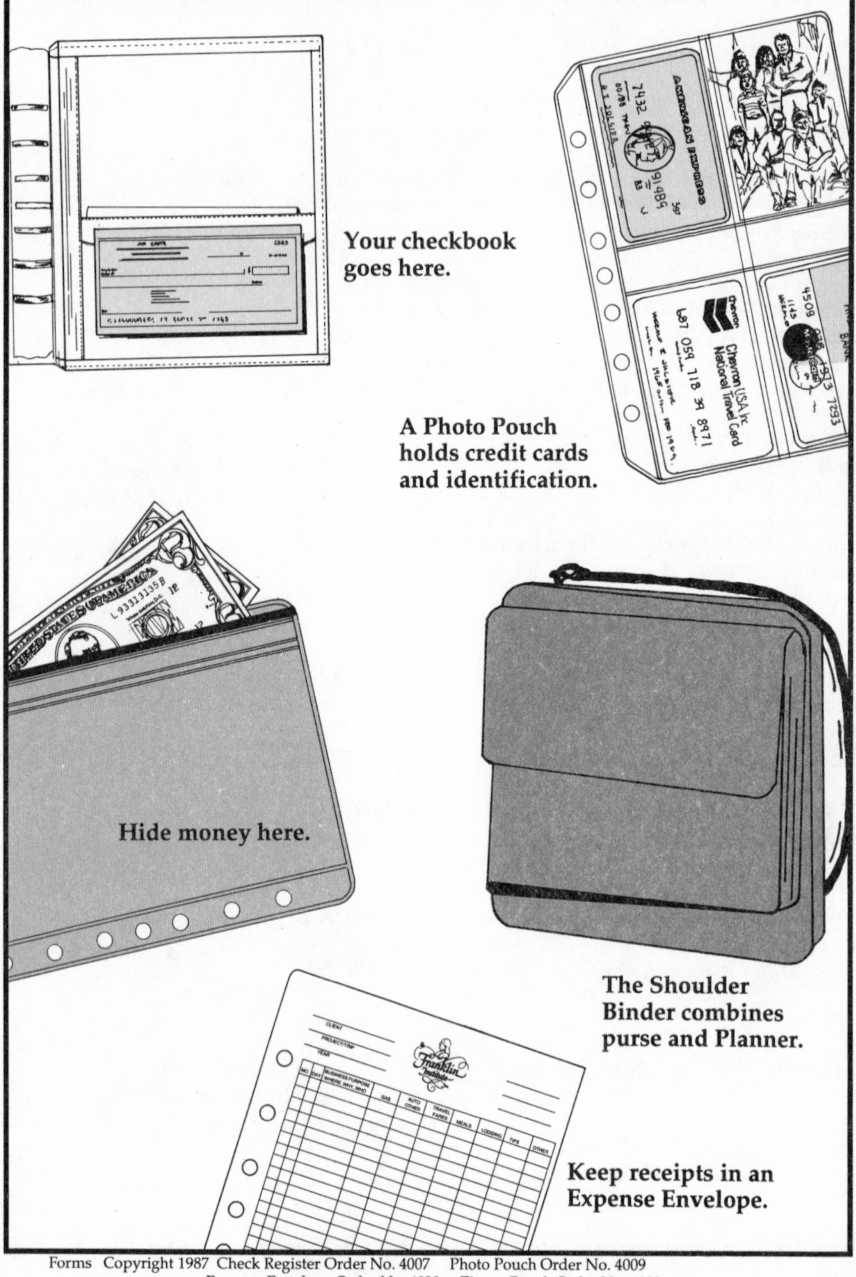

Your checkbook goes here.
A Photo Pouch holds credit cards and identification.
Hide money here.
The Shoulder Binder combines purse and Planner.
Keep receipts in an Expense Envelope.

Forms Copyright 1987 Check Register Order No. 4007 Photo Pouch Order No. 4009
Expense Envelope Order No. 4029 Zipper Pouch Order No. 4008

40

What do you keep in your wallet? Money, credit cards, photos, business cards, checkbook? There is a place for every one of these things in your Franklin binder.

The checkbook slips into the lower back pocket of the binder. The bank register can be kept in the pocket above. Or use the Franklin Check Register—a one-page form that records up to forty-four entries.

Credit cards can be kept in Photo Pouches, eight cards to a page. Business cards and family photos also fit in the Photo Pouch.

Money is easily hidden in the Planner in an Opaque Zipper Pouch. You are the only one who knows there is money in it. Loose change can be kept together in a small, thin coin purse that easily fits in the Zipper Pouch. Some binders (Clutch and Deluxe Presidential Leather styles) have a zipper pocket built in. The Shoulder Binder combines a woman's purse and Planner, and has a large pocket for keys and comb.

If you are one of those that fills your pockets, wallet, or glove box with old receipts, you can now keep those in your Planner as well. The Expense Envelope is perfect for holding a month's receipts.

All this adds less than one quarter inch of bulk to your Planner—thinner than any wallet.

Storage Binder

Storage Binders are like Tupperware—you can store almost anything in them!
NOTEBOOK
STUDY
MEETINGS
JOURNAL
BUSINESS CARDS

Order No. 2109

41

Jane Dalley, a distant relative, loves Tupperware. I guess you could say she is a fanatic. Her kitchen looks like a Tupperware ad. She keeps noodles, tools, sewing supplies, jewelry, chocolate chips, and pies in Tupperware. She even empties new breakfast cereals into specially designed containers.

Blaine Wadman is the same way with Franklin binders. He has bought probably twenty binders from us, all different kinds, all for himself. The curiosity was killing me so I called him yesterday and asked him what he was doing with all those binders. He explained a thorough filing system.

Besides his daily planning binder, he keeps a separate binder strictly for personal journal entries. Another binder serves as a study notebook; any personal study notes go in this binder indexed by book or topic. A Storage Binder holds each month's papers: Daily Record Pages, Meeting Agendas, expense records, journal pages (taken from journal binder at end of month), and study notes. A separate binder, containing Photo Pouches, is an alphabetical index of business cards. Yet another contains Blaine's Prospect Files. And a final Storage Binder holds quotes. That brings us to eighteen binders—he said he has a few extra, just because he likes the way they look.

Blaine has the right idea. A Storage Binder is for storing things—anything you want.

Sources:

Blaine Wadman
Wadman Corporation
Ogden, Utah

Jane Dalley
Biloxi, Mississippi

Meeting Agenda Forms

Write all ideas and agenda items for a meeting on the corresponding Meeting Agenda page—that way everything is together for the meeting.

MEETING PLANNER

Date Schedule 9/20/87
Meeting Title EXEC. MEETING
Purpose
Desired Results
Location

The Franklin Institute Inc.

MEETING PLANNER

Date Schedule 9/11/87
Meeting Title BOARD MEETING
Purpose
Desired Results
Location

The Franklin Institute Inc.

SCHEDULED TIME			ACTUAL TIME			MEETING COST
Start	Stop	Total Hrs.	Start	Stop	Total Hrs.	

Meeting Method	Meeting Type
Facilitator	Recorder
Group Leader	Time Keeper

	Group Members to Attend	Attn.	Value Per Hr.	Total
1				
2				
3				
4				
5				
6				
7				
8				
9				
10				
11				
12				
13				
14				
15				

	Items To Be Discussed (Sequence)	#
1	QUARTERLY REPORT	
2	SALES TO DATE	
3	MARKETING CONVENTION	
4	PERSONNEL—BONUSES	
5	NEW BENEFITS PROGRAM	
6	NEW POLICIES	
7		
8		
9		
10		
11		
12		
13		

2

At lunch the other day, my friend Michael Bingham related this story:

> *I was saying good-bye to our board members after the quarterly meeting, when something someone said reminded me of an agenda item I had neglected to bring up. I was pretty aggravated with myself for having forgotten, because it was an important topic and couldn't wait three months until the next meeting. I spent the next three days on the phone discussing the matter with each board member individually. Not only did this process take a lot of time, it was also more difficult to reach a consensus because we were not all together.*
>
> *I must admit I was chagrined that, in spite of my organization efforts with the Franklin Day Planner, I still forgot something so vital.*

So I told Mike about the Meeting Agenda forms. I keep one Red Tab just for the month's meetings—one form for each meeting. During the month, as I think of agenda items, I write them on the Agenda page for that meeting. That way, I always know where all notes are concerning any meeting.

I spoke again with Mike recently. He showed me the Red Tab full of Meeting Agendas for the next two months, and said he has accomplished more in his meetings since he and his employees began using the Agenda form. "Hyrum," he said, "you've got to really push these Meeting Agendas. I'll tell you, they have made a world of difference in my company, and I recommend them to anyone who attends meetings." Thanks for the plug, Mike.

Source: **Michael J. Bingham**
Bingham and Associates
Ogden, Utah

Close Encounters of the Franklin Kind

The Day Planner can be a great conversation piece.

43

I was in New York City for a meeting with one of our clients whose office is in the World Trade Center. Have you any idea what it's like to be inside the Trade Towers during rush hour? Most buildings don't have a rush hour, but these do.

My appointment was first thing in the morning, so I was shuffling in with all the morning commuters. After waiting for about ten minutes, twenty-five of us piled into an elevator headed for floors fifty and above. I had my Franklin Planner in hand, of course, and as I looked around (what little I could—we were rather crowded), I saw one, two, three . . . at least five other Franklin Planners. I started a conversation with the person nearest me who had a Franklin, and as we talked, others joined in. All told, thirteen of us were carrying Franklin Planners.

We all had a great conversation. As one gentleman and I stepped off the elevator together, he commented that this was the first time he had spoken to anyone on the elevator in two years; the last time was when a lady stepped on his toes with her high heels.

Source: **24 Elevator Companions, New York City, New York**

Rubber Stamps

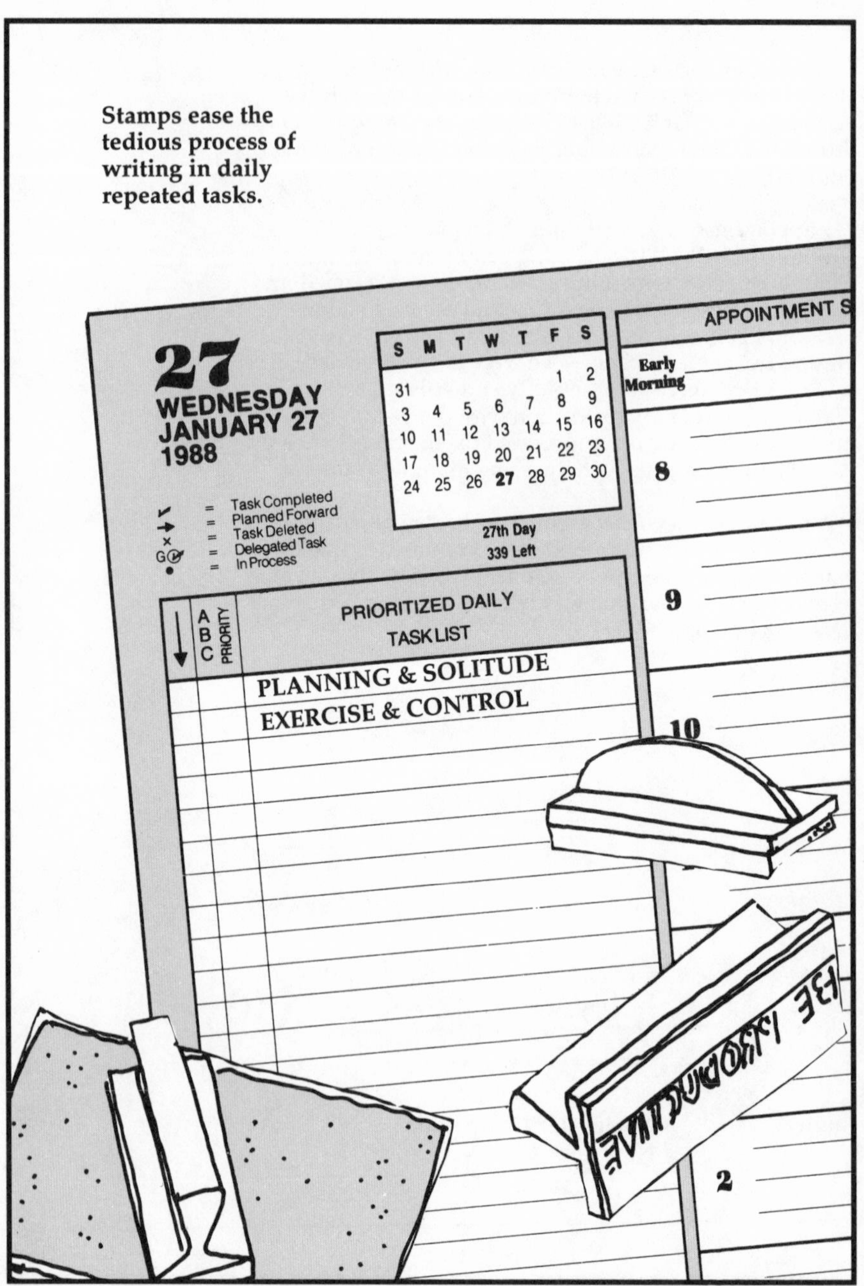

Stamps ease the tedious process of writing in daily repeated tasks.

There are tasks you perform every day: planning and solitude, exercise, daily maintenance tasks, etc. Do you earn a check for these every day? You should. Those checks really feel great.

Tom Young loves checks but hates writing in everyday tasks. He had two rubber stamps prepared for items repeated daily: namely, planning and solitude, and exercise and diet control. He goes through the Planner at the beginning of each month and stamps these tasks in red ink at the head of each Prioritized Daily Task List. He comments, "First, this helps me to remember that I need to dedicate a few minutes to planning. Second, it is easier to stamp it than to have to write it every day."

Have a rubber stamp made for each task repeated daily.

This is a good way to include those personal progress goals that stem from your Productivity Pyramid. If your value says *I Am Healthy,* and your goal states *I Will Exercise For Thirty Minutes Every Day,* that "task" goes in the Daily Task List—every day. Earn a check for it.

There may be several daily activities relating to your value structure which you can stamp instead of write. If the task is written (or stamped) every day, are the chances greater that it will get done? You bet. And what are the chances of your forgetting if it is not written?

Stamping the task for several days or weeks in advance reminds us of personal commitments, and helps us follow through with them. Do you think that will affect our degree of personal satisfaction and self-esteem? Absolutely.

A good way to remind yourself of personal commitments is to stamp or write the task (short-term goal) every day or week.

Source: **Tom Young**
Young Electric Sign Company
Salt Lake City, Utah

Billable Hours

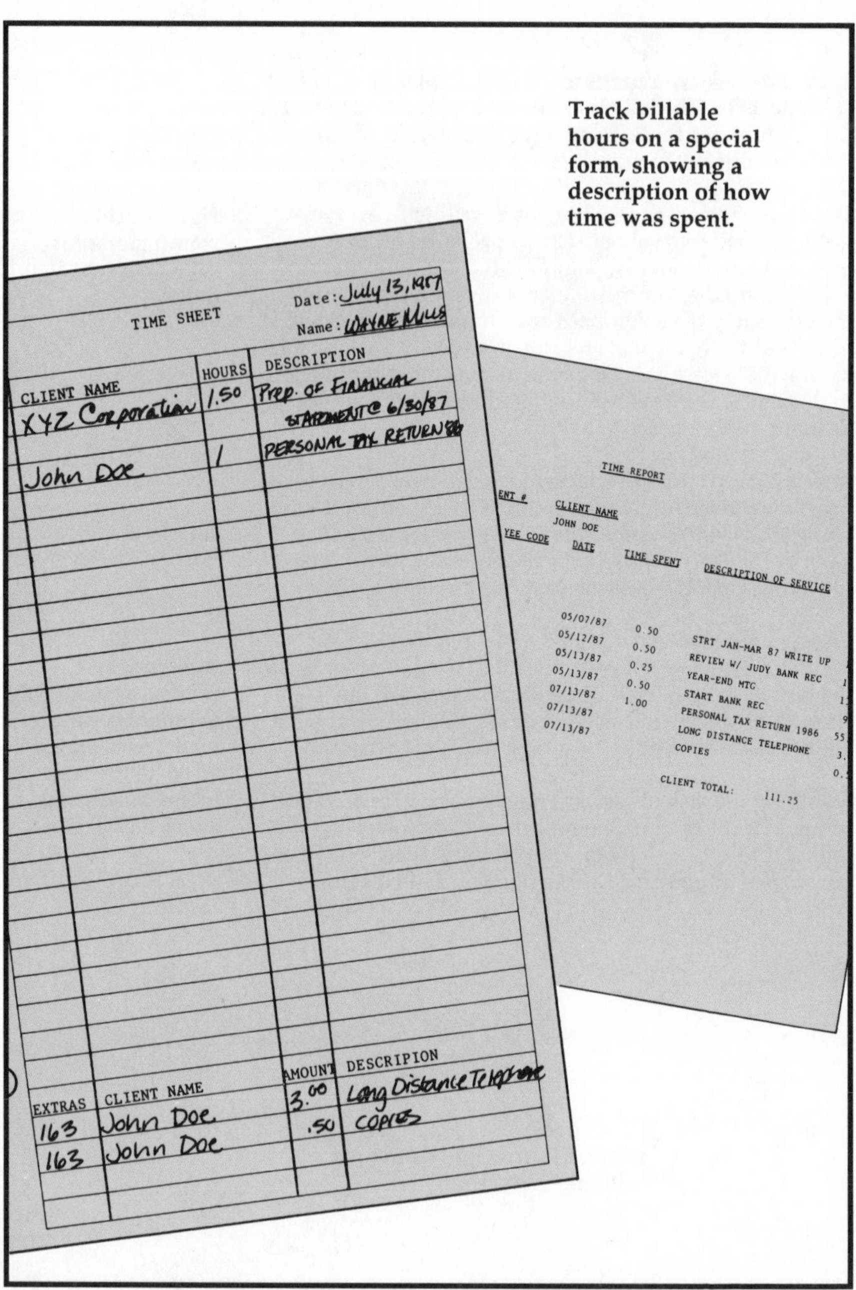

TIME SHEET

Date: July 13, 1987

Name: WAYNE MILLS

CLIENT NAME	HOURS	DESCRIPTION
XYZ Corporation	1.50	Prep. of FINANCIAL STATEMENT @ 6/30/87
John Doe	1	PERSONAL TAX RETURN 86

EXTRAS	CLIENT NAME	AMOUNT	DESCRIPION
163	John Doe	3.00	Long Distance Telephone
163	John Doe	.50	COPIES

TIME REPORT

ENT #

CLIENT NAME

JOHN DOE

YEE CODE

DATE	TIME SPENT	DESCRIPTION OF SERVICE
05/07/87	0.50	STRT JAN-MAR 87 WRITE UP
05/12/87	0.50	REVIEW W/ JUDY BANK REC
05/13/87	0.25	YEAR-END MTC
05/13/87	0.50	START BANK REC
07/13/87	1.00	PERSONAL TAX RETURN 1986
07/13/87		LONG DISTANCE TELEPHONE
07/13/87		COPIES

CLIENT TOTAL: 111.25

Track billable hours on a special form, showing a description of how time was spent.

When the attorney's bill came in the mail, Wayne was astounded. A thousand dollars—why so much? The only comment on the statement was, "Thank you for your prompt payment."

Because of that experience, Wayne Mills, CPA, developed a billing system for his own office that justifies the amount billed. It includes a Billable Hours form for the Day Planner, and a computer software program that makes the billing process much easier on himself, his secretary, and especially, his clients.

When Wayne completes a task for which a client will be billed, he fills out the Billable Hours form with client number and name, how much time he spent, and a description of what he was doing. At the end of each day, this sheet goes to his secretary for data entry in the computer. All this information appears on the client's monthly statement, including a brief description of services performed.

Wayne said his collection problems have been reduced substantially since he began including descriptions of time use on the statement. And his secretary loves the daily Billable Hours form—it shortens time spent preparing statements for mailing.

Recording billable hours daily eases the burden during billing time.

Source: **Wayne Mills**
W. S. Mills and Co., CPAs
Salt Lake City, Utah

Weekly Master Task List

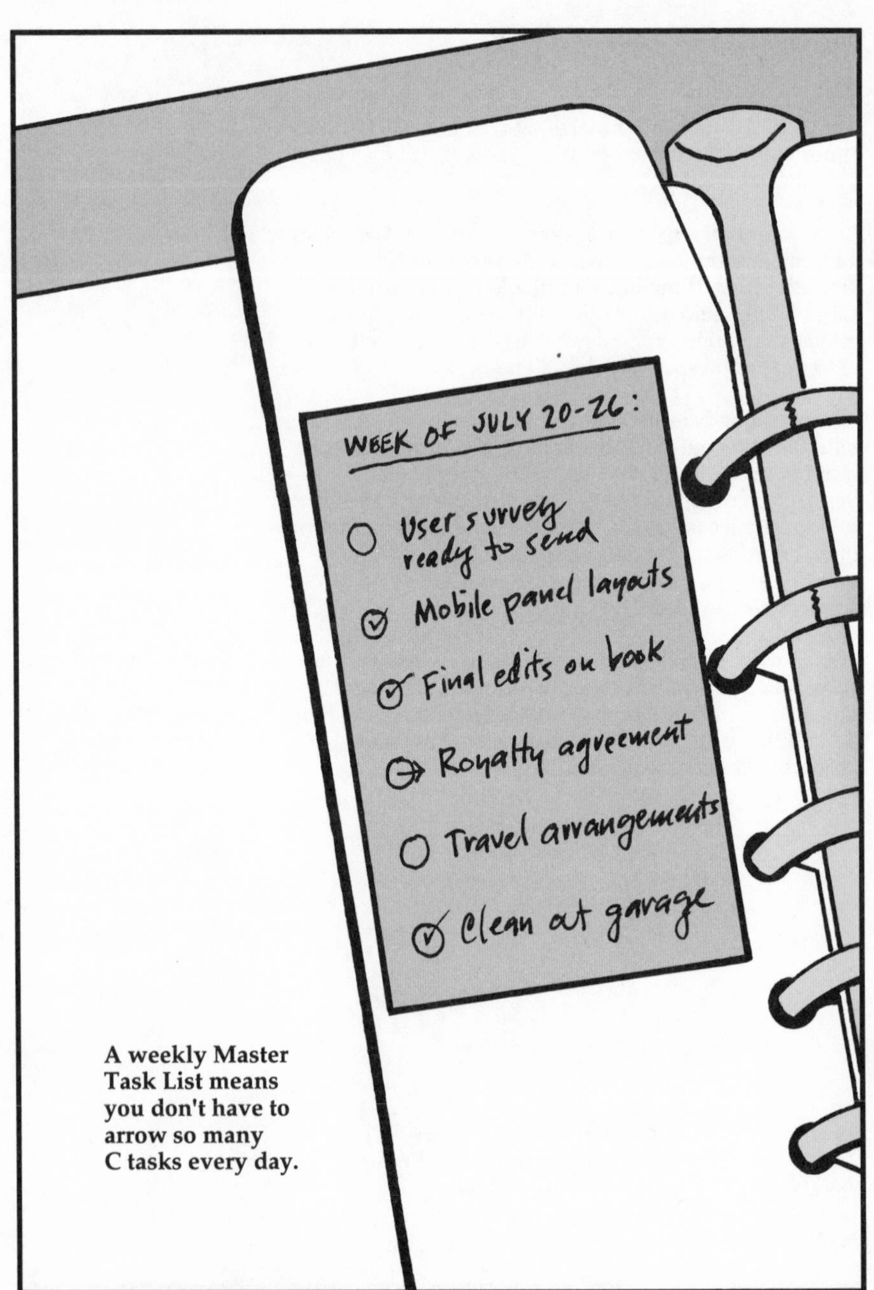

A weekly Master Task List means you don't have to arrow so many C tasks every day.

46

The monthly Master Task List is a good place to write any task that doesn't have a date or a deadline. Sometimes we don't really care if it gets done—like clean the garage. But it's nice to have it on a list somewhere.

Other times it is important to complete these tasks. Jerry Pulsipher likes to make sure he gets them done (he has the cleanest garage I have ever seen). Instead of writing on the Master Task List page, which he rarely refers to, he keeps a weekly Master Task List stuck to his Day Finder. A sticky note page works well. Because it is only for one week, this list isn't very long. He uses the same symbols as on the Daily Task List to mark his progress. The list could also be prioritized, but Jerry says he is too "right-brained" for that.

When he thinks of something to do next week, he slips a sticky note in on the following Monday's page and begins a new Master Task List. When this week is over, he plans forward unfinished tasks, and replaces the old list with the new one (already begun). The list is always in front of him, reminding him of important tasks. It also saves him from planning forward those C priorities all week long.

By the way, Don Wilhelm sent me this definition:

> *Master Task List: All the things you want to do, but can't do right now, might do tomorrow, could do next week, but hope to do during the month.*

Sources: **Jerry Pulsipher**
The Franklin Institute, Inc.
Salt Lake City, Utah

Don Wilhelm
Layton, Utah

The Rigby Bag

FOR THE FANATICAL FEW

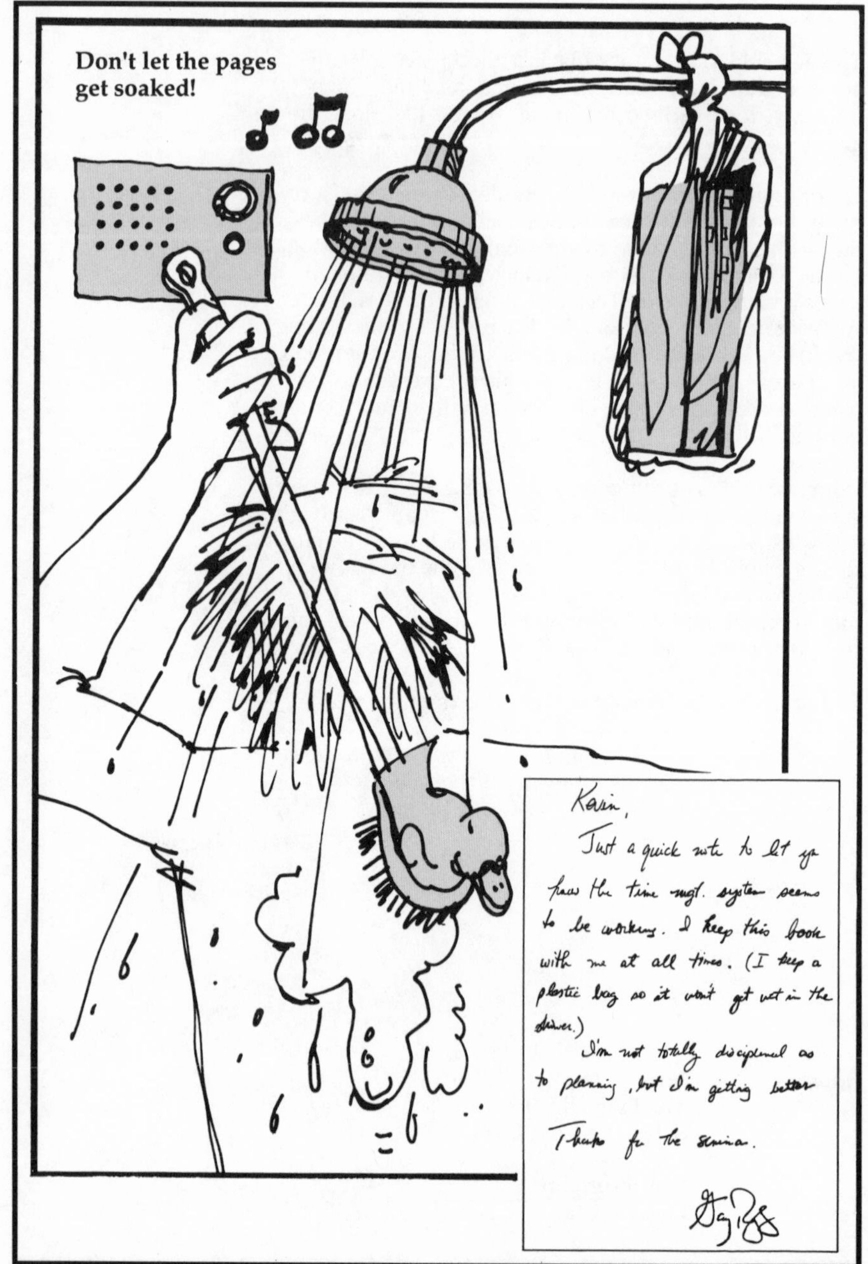

Kevin,

Just a quick note to let you know the time mgt. system seems to be working. I keep this book with me at all times. (I keep a plastic bag so it won't get wet in the shower.)

I'm not totally disciplined as to planning, but I'm getting better.

Thanks for the seminar.

This novel idea is only for real enthusiasts.

Gary Rigby takes his Planner in the shower with him! Not every day, only on days when he has a little time and might get a terrific inspiration. Kevin asked him how he avoids getting the pages wet. He said it requires a lot of finesse; you must learn to kind of dance around so that when the water changes direction, the pages are still protected. When he's not writing in it, he keeps it next to his radio. He must be one of those who get their best ideas in the shower. Personally, I prefer to sing in the shower.

Actually, the idea is to keep your Planner with you at all times—or at least nearby. I usually get my best ideas at night, about 2:00 or 3:00 a.m. I used to spend half the night worrying that I might forget it by morning, and the entire next morning trying to remember what the great idea was that kept me up half the night.

When do you get your best ideas? Is your Planner there with you?

Now my Planner is always close by, on the nightstand if there's room. When I get a good idea, or a not-so-good idea (they all seem good at 3:00 in the morning), I write it down in full detail in my Planner. By that time, I'm tired and fall right to sleep, with the right to "forget" until morning.

Source: **Gary Rigby**
Merrill Lynch
Ocala, Florida

Alphabet Tabs

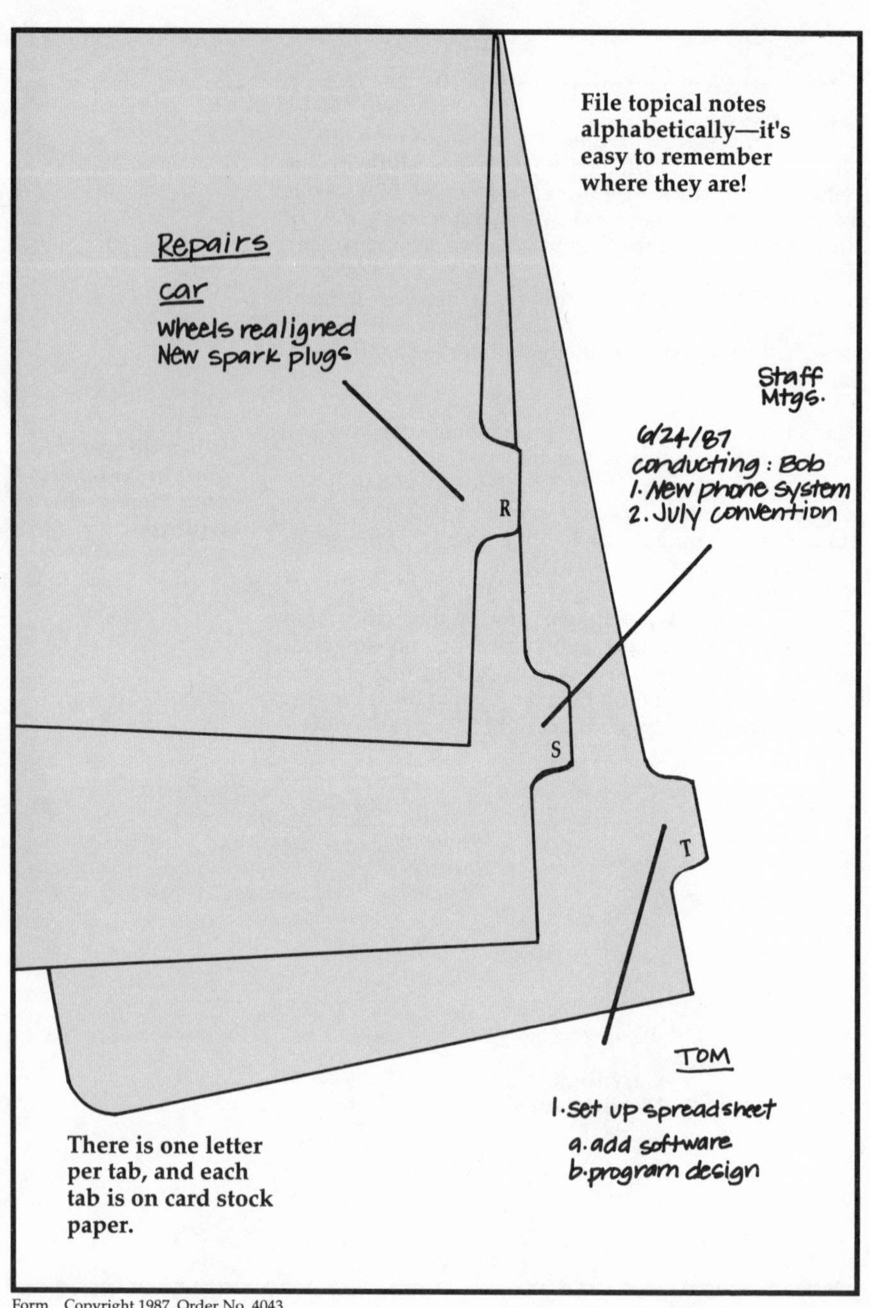

File topical notes alphabetically—it's easy to remember where they are!
Repairs
car
wheels realigned
New spark plugs
R
Staff Mtgs.
6/24/87
conducting : Bob
1. New phone system
2. July convention
S
T
TOM
1. set up spreadsheet
a. add software
b. program design
There is one letter per tab, and each tab is on card stock paper.

48

For some reason, it feels good to file things alphabetically. That's why The Franklin Institute, Inc., now makes Alphabet Tabs.

Originally, they were created for a prospect or client file. Whether kept in the Day Planner binder or in a separate one, a client file needs to be alphabetized (see idea 10). If you are managing many projects, the project files can also be filed alphabetically.

Jesslyn Hilt has developed an alphabetical index method; instead of using the six Red Tabs that come with the Planner, she uses Alphabet Tabs. She takes notes from a meeting or conversation on lined paper and files them alphabetically. Staff meeting notes go under "S"; repairs under "R"; projects she is helping people with go under the person's first initial. The Alphabet Tabs give her greater capacity for filing categorically than the six or even the eighteen Red Tabs.

Alphabetical filing almost eliminates the need for filling out the Monthly Index pages. Since she records only one-time events on the Daily Record of Events page, there is very little information to record on the Index page. Everything she may need to refer back to is filed alphabetically.

Source: **Jesslyn Hilt**
Federal Home Loan Bank of Seattle
Seattle, Washington

Shopping List

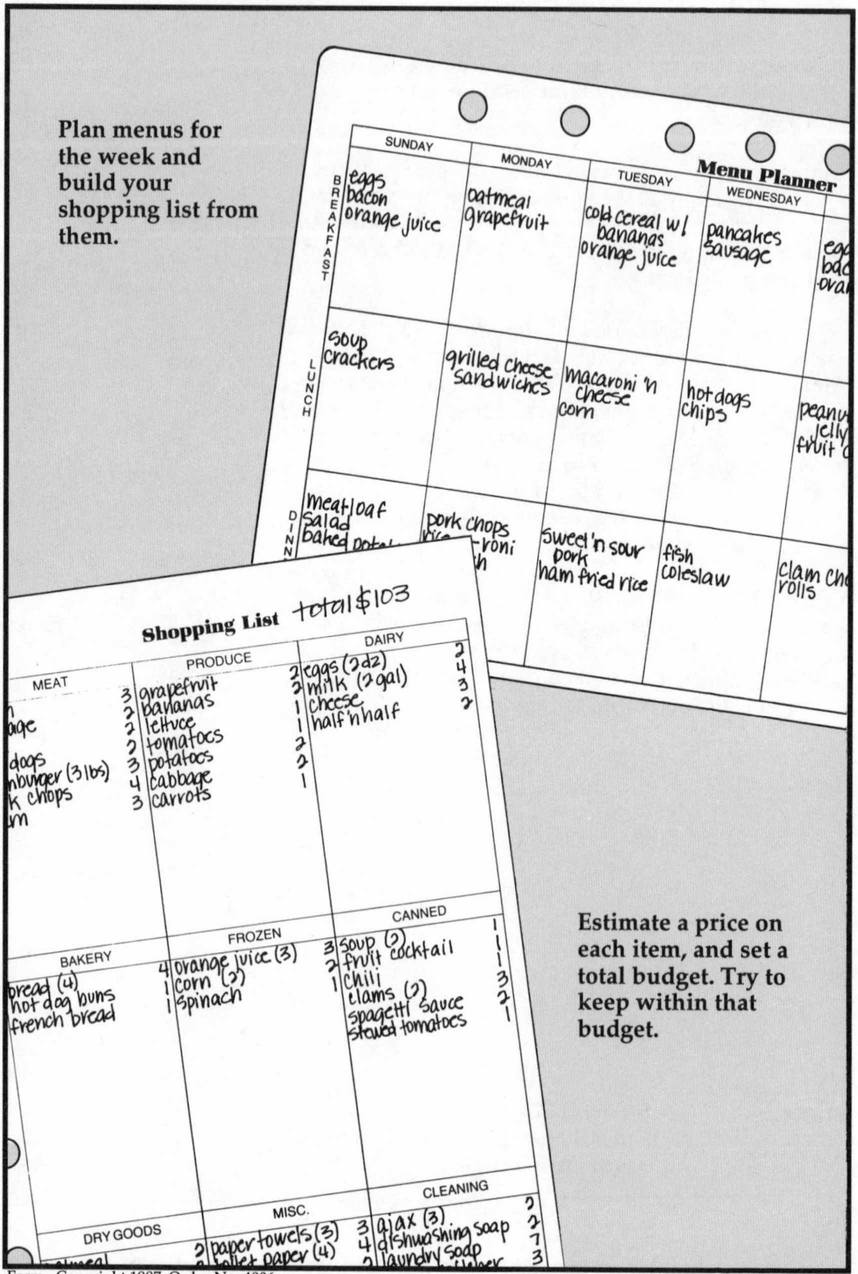

Plan menus for the week and build your shopping list from them.

Estimate a price on each item, and set a total budget. Try to keep within that budget.

I'm going to talk about my secretary, Colleen, again. I wouldn't mention her so much if she weren't so scary with her Planner!

Colleen used to spend half her paycheck every time she went to the grocery store. To break herself of this habit she bought some Shopping Lists for her Planner. The front side is a categorized shopping list, and the back is a weekly menu planner. Colleen explains how she uses it:

> *First, I plan menus for the week. Since I work full time, this makes life much easier for me and my family. Then I list any items needed for those meals. During the week, I list other items as I notice they are getting low. Before going to the grocery store, I estimate how much each product will cost, and budget a total amount for that shopping trip.*
>
> *My goal is to keep at or below the budget. I usually spend about five dollars less than I had estimated. This system helps me control impulse buying, which results in a lower budget and healthier foods for my family.*

Now, how many people do you know who are that creative with their shopping list?

Source: **Colleen Dom**
Marketing Assistant
The Franklin Institute, Inc.

Travel Bonuses

AIRLINE MILES - 1987

	FROM - TO	DATE	LINE	MILES	CUM	VAL	DEL
1	PDX - ORD	1-5	VAL	1739		48925	7615
2	ORD - LGA	1-5	"	750			
3	LGA - BWI	1-7	"	750			
4	BWI - ORD	1-9	"	750			
5	ORD - PDX	1-9	"	1739	102525		
6	PDX - LAX	1-12	ALASKA	839			
7	LAX - PHX	1-13	VAL	750			
8	PHX - SLC	1-14	SW	540			
9	SLC - PDX	1-15	DELTA	1000			8615
10	PDX - ORD	1-19	UAL	1739			
11	ORD - BOS	1-19	"	750			
12	BOS - DEN	1-21	"	1625			
13	DEN - PDX	1-21	"	985	110753	58763	
14	PDX - SEA	1-27	NWEST	500			
15	SEA - PDX	1-28	ALASKA	500			
16	PDX - SFO	2-3	VAL	750			
17	SFO - SLC	2-5	"	750			
18	SLC - PDX	2-6	DELTA	840			945
19	PDX - ORD	2-9	VAL	1739			
20	ORD - IAD	2-9	"	750			
21	IAD - LAX	2-11	AA	2385			
22	LAX - PDX	2-13	ALASKA	981	119948		
23	PDX - SFO	2-16	UAL	750			
24	SFO - HKG	2-16	"	7835			
25	HKG - SFO	2-26	"	78			
26	SFO - PDX	2-26	"				
27							
28							
29							
30							
31							

FREQUENT FLYE
0004032266
DENNY R. JON

Track mileage and bonus points on a 13 Column Spread Sheet and compare with monthly travel club statement.

Frequent Flyer, One Pass, Mileage Plus, Advantage. Bonus points, first class upgrades, discounts on ticket fares. Stay at the right hotels, drive the right rental cars, eat at certain restaurants, and you get more for your money.

Travel clubs are very popular these days, and can help save you a lot of money, if you do it right. Keeping track of where to stay and where to rent your car to earn points with the right airline, however, can be tricky.

Brian Horan of Coopers and Lybrand travels frequently. In order to capitalize on all the discounts, he keeps schedules (by airline) of hotels, car rentals, and other services that earn bonus points.

Dick Winwood, a trainer at the Franklin, keeps track of his flight mileage and services used (hotel, car, etc.) on a 13 Column Spread Sheet. For every trip he records the mileage and bonus points accrued, then compares this monthly sheet with his travel club statement. He has found many discrepancies this way.

It must pay off, because Dick recently took his family to Hong Kong and paid nothing for the airline tickets!

Sources:

Brian Horan
Coopers and Lybrand
Newark, New Jersey

Dick Winwood
The Franklin Institute, Inc.
Portland, Oregon

The Family Constitution

The Constitution will serve as a guideline for both individual and family goal setting and planning.

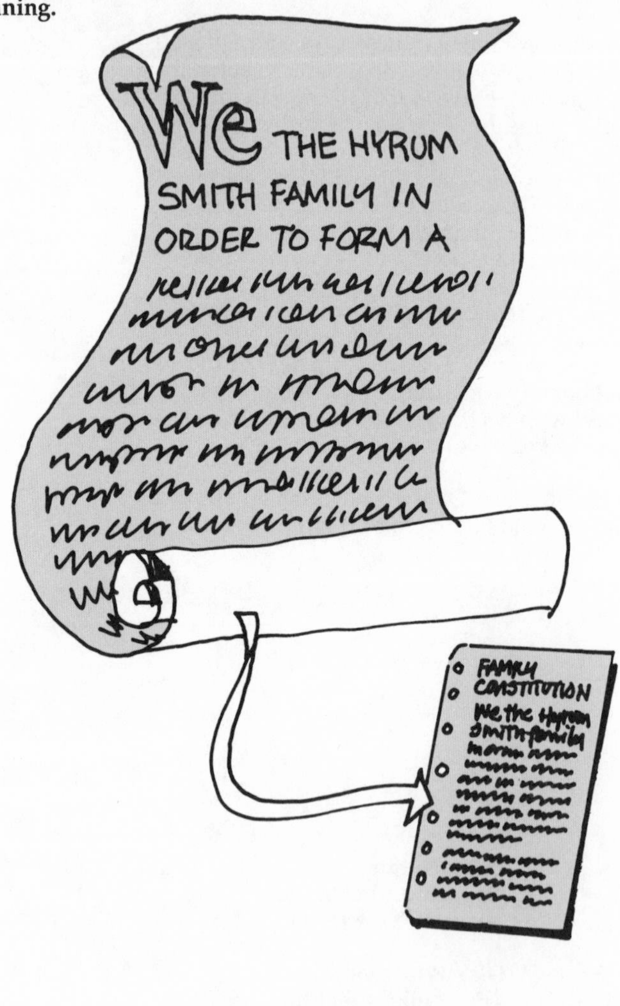

One of the world's greatest government documents was created by a group of statesmen and colonizers who had absolutely no experience in setting up forms of government. But they knew how they wanted to live—they had a goal. The result of the dreams of these men was the Constitution of the United States.

A Family Constitution is a mission statement: what the family wants to become and why.

Just as from the Constitution grew one of the world's strongest nations, I submit that your family can also become an organization for the betterment of its members, and those who interact with them, through developing and following a Family Constitution.

Writing a Family Constitution is an opportunity to meet as a family and get the candid input of each member. Start by identifying family values: ask "What do we want as a family? How do we want to feel while together? What kind of atmosphere shall we create?"

Each member should contribute.

Then decide how to make these values happen in your family by asking questions such as: "What goals would we like to achieve as a family? How can this family structure contribute to individual goals? How can individuals advance the progress of the family goals? Which laws and rights need to be established in order to encourage individual and family development?"

Your Family Constitution is a guideline for family goal setting. Intermediate and short-term goals will stem from and support its articles.

The Constitution will serve as a guideline for both individual and family goal setting and planning.

You may find, as our family has, that identifying and writing down family values and goals clarifies the purpose of having families, gives specific purpose to your family unit, and fosters cooperation and respect among all its members.

Source: **The Hyrum Smith Family**
Centerville, Utah

Recurring Monthly Events

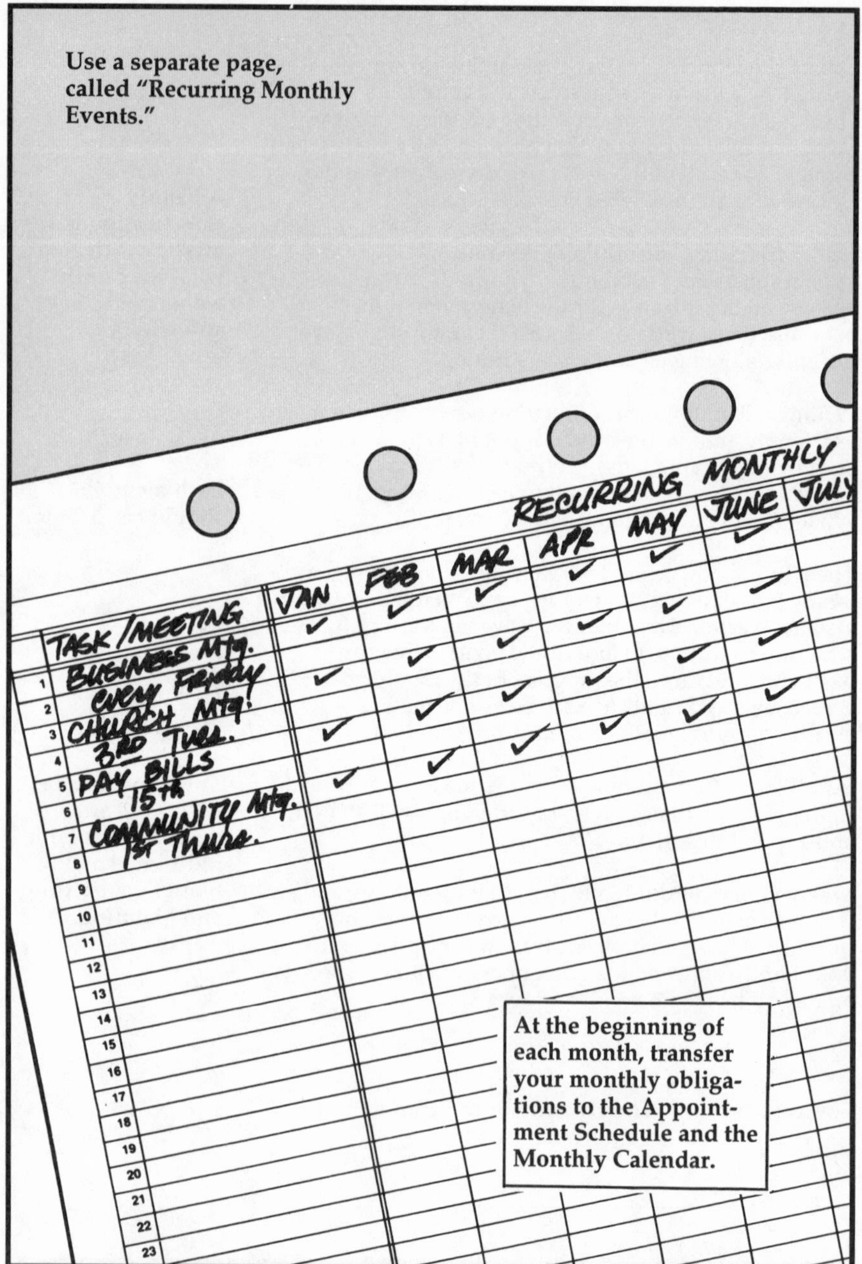

Use a separate page, called "Recurring Monthly Events."
RECURRING MONTHLY
TASK/MEETING
JAN
FEB
MAR
APR
MAY
JUNE
JULY
BUSINESS Mtg. every Friday
CHURCH Mtg. 3RD TUES.
PAY BILLS 15th
COMMUNITY Mtg. 1st Thurs.
At the beginning of each month, transfer your monthly obligations to the Appointment Schedule and the Monthly Calendar.

52

One of my friends is a member of an organization that meets the first Wednesday of each month. He has forgotten at least two meetings that I know of because he neglected to write that monthly event in his daily Appointment Schedule and Monthly Calendar pages.

He should use Dave Burton's idea. Dave keeps a Recurring Monthly Events page which lists all monthly meetings and obligations. The form is at the front of his Planner. At the beginning of each month he fills in these obligations on the Daily Appointment Schedule and Monthly Calendar.

I'll bet Dave never misses a lodge meeting.

Source: **Dave Burton**
UNISYS
Salt Lake City, Utah

Mom's Planner: the Family Organizer

Each family member writes in Mom's Planner when they need her help.

In the midst of what seemed to be another typical family mix-up, Shary Davidson discovered a way to organize and coordinate her family's activities: everything must be recorded in her Planner.

Passing the buck is difficult when the commitment is recorded in the Planner.

Shary records whatever is discussed in her Planner, and alongside is the name of whoever is responsible for the tasks. This makes follow-up easier and passing the buck nearly impossible.

Younger children have regular planning meetings with Mom.

If her sixteen-year-old daughter wants Shary to do something, it must be written in Shary's Day Planner so that she is fairly informed. If it isn't written in the Planner, she isn't expected to respond. Likewise, anything Shary would like her children or husband to do for her also goes in the Planner. Shary takes special time for planning with the two younger ones at home, and they love having "grown-up" planning sessions with their mom.

This system of communication has lightened her heavy load of responsibility for everyone's activities. It also eliminates grumbling, whining, creative excuse making, and low self-image. Shary comments, "As a working wife and mother, I know I am juggling overlapping schedules considerably better. Best of all, priorities are more quickly identified. I can spot the light at the end of the tunnel almost immediately! I am more creative, more enthused, more motivated, more productive. And I am receiving more hugs!"

Source: **Shary Davidson**
Grand Junction, Colorado

Survival in a New City

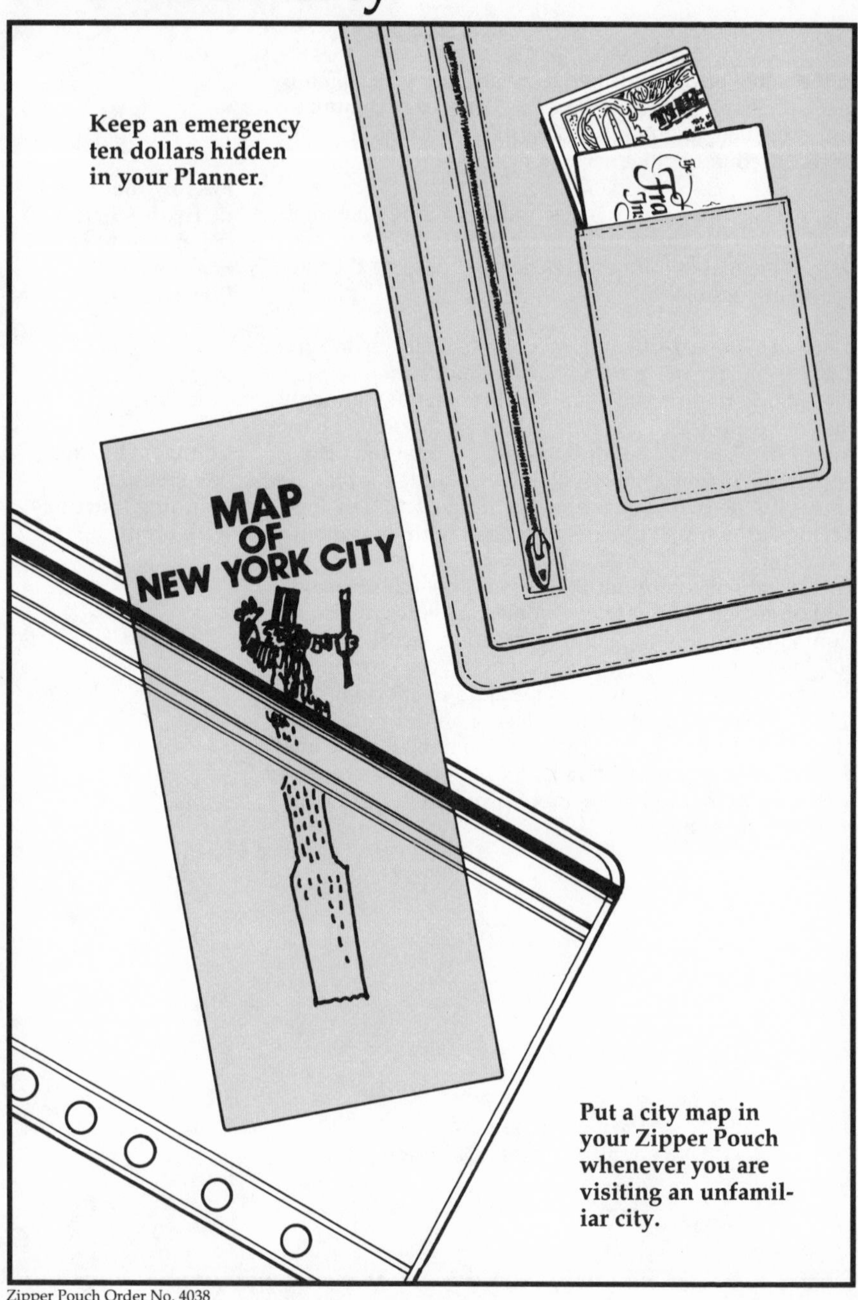

Keep an emergency ten dollars hidden in your Planner.

Put a city map in your Zipper Pouch whenever you are visiting an unfamiliar city.

Zipper Pouch Order No. 4038

54

On the flight from Salt Lake to New York, Dennis Webb wanted to watch the James Bond movie, "Never Say Never Again." He asked Lynn Robbins to loan him the three dollars. Reluctantly, Lynn loaned him the money—Dennis loved the movie.

In New York, they rented a car and headed for Ithaca. Approaching the first toll, Lynn asked Dennis if he had brought the petty cash for the tolls. "No," said Dennis, "you were supposed to bring it."

"I thought we agreed that *you* would bring it," answered Lynn. "I *had* three dollars."

They pulled up to the toll booth.

"You don't have any money?" asked the cashier.

"No sir—but will you take a credit card?" Dennis asked.

"Back up and turn around."

Taking the first exit, they landed in the heart of the Bronx, where they began searching for a gas station that would cash an out-of-state check. Two and a half hours later, they found one. But by then, they were so lost that they spent another two hours finding a way out!

Fortunately, they were not late for their morning appointment—they only missed one night's sleep.

Dennis offers two bits of advice for travelers, so they don't repeat this scenario: (1) Don't forget toll money! But because that's easier said than done, keep an emergency ten dollars hidden in your binder somewhere (like Lynn *now* does!). (2) Keep a city map in the binder whenever you are visiting a new city. Car rental agencies usually have maps that fit nicely in a Zipper Pouch.

Sources: **Dennis Webb**
Lynn Robbins
The Franklin Institute, Inc.
Salt Lake City, Utah

Directory of Directions

ADDRESS PHONE DIRECTORY

F

NAME	ADDRESS	PHONE
First State Bank	3391 So. Pioneer Dr.	555-1000

First State Bank

Take Highway 80 to 3300. Turn Left to 300 East. Turn right to Pioneer Dr.

Write directions on a sticky note and keep in the Address/Phone section for future reference.

55

A friend of mine, Bob Rogers, recently moved to Salt Lake City from San Francisco. I guess Salt Lake's orderly grid system for city planning is too much for someone from a place like San Francisco; Bob had only been here a month and had already called me three times for directions to the same place. I don't know who he calls when I'm not in town, but I feel sorry for them. So for his birthday, I gave Bob a Franklin Planner and the following suggestion that comes from Owen Zuro.

When he moved to Cleveland three years ago, Owen didn't know his way around at all. When people gave him directions, he threw them away after using them once. But the next time he wanted to go to the same place, he was stuck! Now, when he gets directions from someone, he writes them on a sticky note and puts the note in his address section under the name of the place. The directions are always with him. When he doesn't need the directions anymore, he tosses the note. Owen also keeps a city map in his Planner.

I guess Bob is doing okay with this idea, because he hasn't called me lately.

Source: **Owen Zuro**
Westlake, Ohio

Priority Codes

Additional priority codes accentuate task categories, making them easier to find.

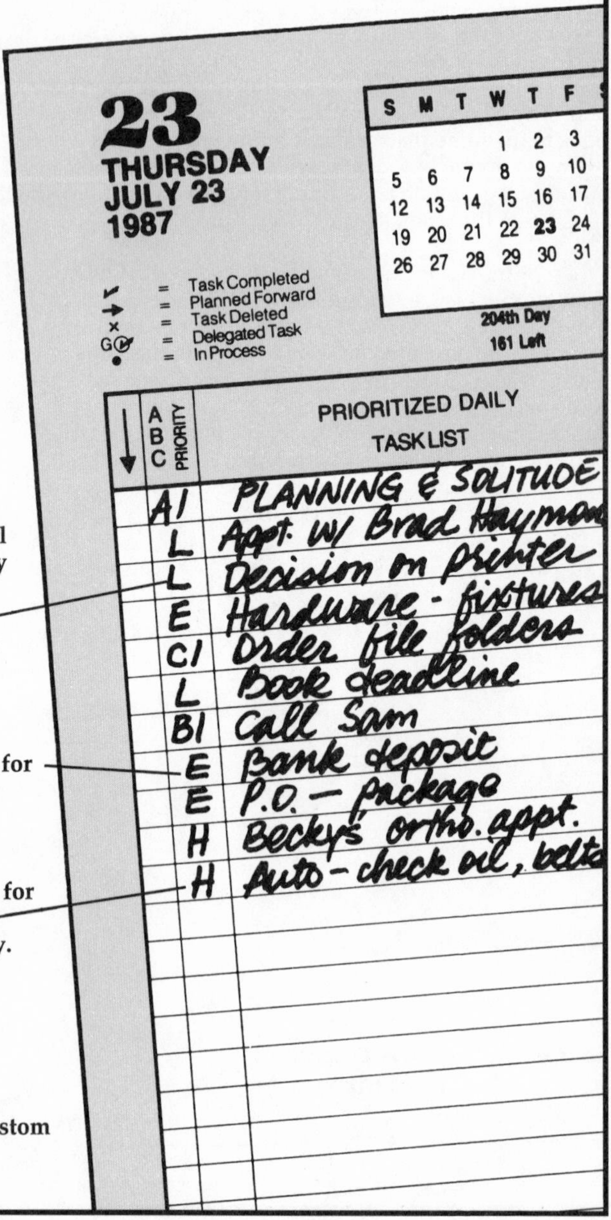

A person's initial used as a priority code, indicates items to be discussed with that individual.

Use an "E" code for errands.

"H" can be used for tasks related to home and family.

Create your own custom priority codes.

56

There have been times when my A tasks could not be done first. For example, one day my A1 task was to speak with Bob (Franklin's president), but Bob was out of the office until 2:00 that afternoon. All morning that A1 bothered me. Other times, my A1's and A2's have been personal projects—responsibilities at home or elsewhere—that I cannot accomplish until after work. I don't feel very much peace on those days until I can check off my A tasks.

Many people have sent in ideas to solve this problem. Here are a few of them:

James Alexander has added the code "E" for errands. He prioritizes the E's according to location, if he has enough time to do them all, or by value.

An "H" code can be used for tasks performed only at home. Jim Bentley begins this list from the bottom of the Daily Task List, and prioritizes the items separately.

Dan Bates needed an easier and faster way to locate items to be discussed with his boss. He uses "L" for his manager, Larry Rhodes. Thus, he quickly locates all discussion items, and gets everything said even when Larry is on the run.

These additional priority codes accentuate task categories, making items easier to find in a long task list. They also allow for prioritizing tasks that can be done only at a certain time of day. And they can give greater inner peace!

Sources:

James Alexander
Job Service
Sandy, Utah

Dan Bates
Job Service
Provo, Utah

Jim Bentley
General Motors Corp.
Saginaw, Michigan

Red Tabs

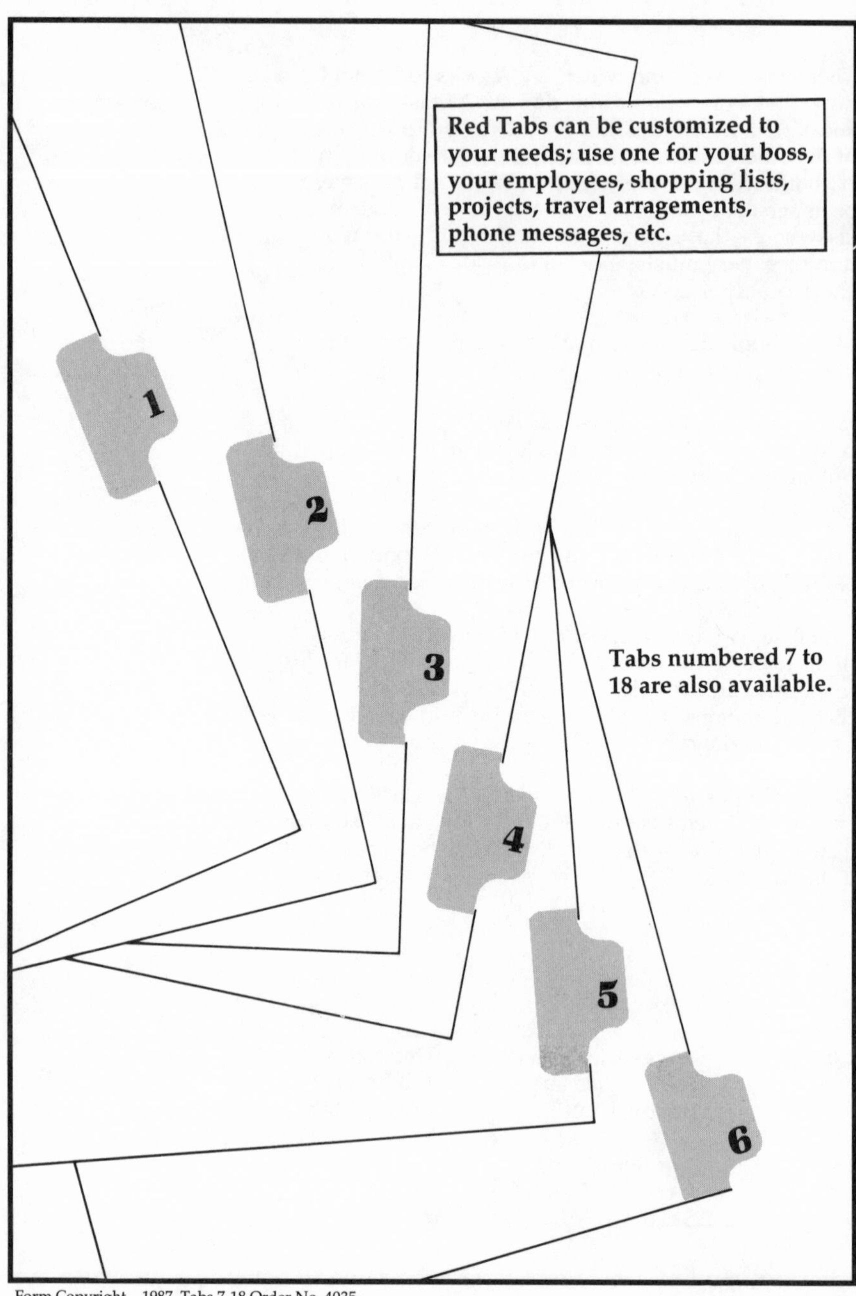

Red Tabs can be customized to your needs; use one for your boss, your employees, shopping lists, projects, travel arragements, phone messages, etc.
1
2
3
4
5
6
Tabs numbered 7 to 18 are also available.

 Tabs 7-18 Order No. 4035

Use Red Tabs to further organize your Planner.

The best thing about the Red Tab section of the Franklin Planner is the organization it affords: topical information is in one place, not scattered throughout the book. Six Tabs come with the Master Filler Set for the Planner. They can be assigned and reassigned at will for various projects.

Randy Young writes that he devotes one tab to employee communications: one page as a Master Task List for each person. Everything pertaining to his subordinates goes behind Red Tab #1, rather than on various daily pages.

Lynette Noble keeps Shopping List pages (see idea 49) and a Christmas shopping list behind one Red Tab. The lists are always with her. The Christmas gift ideas she has in June are recorded in her Planner and ready for action come the holiday season.

Any long-term project deserves a Red Tab. Keeping track of what needs to be done and what has been done is difficult at best when coordinating efforts of several people in several functions. Having every note on the project in one place simplifies the whole process.

Ongoing files are nice to keep behind a Red Tab. Children's records, a list of books to read, and journal entries are just a few of the things that we usually want to remember but rarely write down—the Planner is the perfect place!

Sources:

Randy Young
R.K. Young Electric
Salt Lake City, Utah

Lynette Noble
St. George, Utah

Monthly Index

JUNE INDEX 1987

Date	Index to important ideas, events, thoughts, etc., that have been recorded.
1	Central Book — "send to" List
	Industrial Show #'s
2	Store: Books to order
	Norma Richardson: Right/Left Brain study
3	Sewing Patterns
6	San Francisco Outlet Shopping
8	Coopers - copier supply prices
	Edna - meeting list
11	Glen Davis - Clipper imprint +.25
12	Dr. Lattener
15	Ken O'Connell
	Bill Baber
	Revere Ware List
16	Glen Davis
	Fancy Plants prices
17	Uphill Down
	Glen Davis - calculators/clocks
	Zoo w/ Kelly & Jordan
18	Don Perry - handwriting
22	Contacts for pg finder in catalog
	Meyer #
23	Eric Anderson
	Pens - #'s and prices
	Jerry - Nebraska
	Tom Parker "Thos"
24	City delivery
	Thos address
	Dr. Eric Anderson - endorphines
	UPS Marty Ryan
25	Glen Davis samples
	Plays in London
26	Glen - Clock w/ alarm
	Uphill Down - grey cordura p[…]
27	hours
29	Ida Smith re. 8/27
	JD - Purses ordered
	Purses - #'s & prices
30	Carolyn Palmer

1 Keep past Monthly Indexes in your Planner.

1986

1987

2 Keep Storage Binders wherever you need the information most.

Storage Binder Order No. 2109

58

In a meeting, Kathy Stuart's boss unexpectedly asked her to report on a transaction that took place three months previously. Kathy was back in the meeting within one minute with all the information. She could do that because of the way she uses her Monthly Index pages.

The Monthly Index is a table of contents for each month.

The Monthly Index is like a table of contents for each month. It is a quick reference guide to everything annotated in the Daily Record of Events pages.

Whenever Kathy has a spare moment (waiting at the doctor's office, riding in the car), she fills in the Monthly Index. That way it is almost always up-to-date.

In her Planner, she keeps Monthly Indexes for the past three or four months for quick reference. She keeps her Storage Binders at work because that is where she usually needs them.

When her boss asked her to find information from three months back, she checked in the Monthly Index for that month, and found the information in her Storage Binder. Her boss was impressed.

Source: **Kathy Stuart**
The Franklin Institute, Inc.
Salt Lake City, Utah

Major Project Forms

Don't forget to first identify the objective or goal.

MAJOR PROJECT

NO. 21

TITLE: BUILDING OUR NEW DREAM HOME

SPECIFIC RESULTS/OBJECTIVE: 4 bedroom home, on 1 acre wooded property. Good School approx 3500 ft Finish by Dec. 1989.

RESULTS MAINTAINANCE PROGRAM: Less than $200K.

PROJECTED COMPLETION: 12-25-89

ASSIGNED TO: AJW/KJW | DATE: 4-20-85 | ACTUAL COMPLETION:

PROJECT MGR: AJW | ASSISTED BY: KJW

PROJECTS MEETING SCHEDULE

KEY TASKS, IDEAS, AND ACTIVITIES	DELEGATED TO	DATE DUE	ACT. ACCOMP. DATE
Chicken wire Red & Black paper in Mud room (See Woodward)	KJ		
Put in a phone Booth 2½ x 2½ upstairs in Hall	AW		
Chisel #'s into granite stone at entrance to drwy.	AW		
Secure interest rate 30 yr. fixed less than 10% 2 ions	AW		
Put Shelfs on wall going down to Basement.	KJ		
See "Contempo" Brand Ceramic tile	KJ		
Use Pella or Anderson wood windows	AW		
Use Stucco By Webber Bros. Dan or Mike	AW		
For Oak rails and crowns call Hal Hudson 467-9888	KJ		
CK-out Stone walls on 13th E. between 13-15 So.	KJ		
Put plug outside for X-mas lights	AW		
raised dening room 4" from Living space	KJ		
look into Sports Courts 972-0080	AW		
CK-out drive way in stone from 49 street gallivia	AW		
Have Covered deck over patio area	AW		
Have red brick Boarding sidewalk	KJ		
Be at Building site when hole is dug.	AW		
CK out Col. Bird plaza at Airport Intern'l Center	AW		
Builders: Con Jensen and Bros.	AW		
Gene Glover Builder 942-8888 (Jeff's Dad)	(Ron)		
Doug Olsen Contractor 579-5990 532-2288	AW		
See outside windows on old home in Ogd. Wall's Riverdale	KJ		
Stucco & Stone 592-4998 Jeff Farrington.	KJ		
Richard Burton $40/ft in Book.	AW		
Fireplace mantel at SL Antiques Ted 489-9289 $1800	Cindi		
Lot From Terra America Don Brady 988-8488	AW	3/86	3/86
Have top soil hauled in Jim Anlt 574-8988	AW	3/87	4/87
Dick Argyle construction took dirt.	AW	4/87	4/87
Get plan Bids Design Masters, Tuttle Soffee Alread	AW	6/87	

Track all tasks on one page.

Alan Wheatley writes:

From time to time a major project comes along, be it work or personal, that will carry out over a period of time (several months or even years).

As with any event or activity, a specific result or objective should be defined, especially when the project involves a boss/subordinate relationship. Clearly defined goals on the project are essential. I created this Major Project Form to track all tasks. I've used Major Project Forms in the past to do many things:

1. *Repairs and items for my car*
2. *List of materials, designs, contractors, etc., for my new home*
3. *Advertising campaign*
4. *"Book"—I'm writing a book. Each time I think of something to include, I write it down.*
5. *New business ideas*

This form works well for me; it helps me see my progress and motivates me to continue working on the project to completion.

A Major Project Form can be used for any long-term project.

Source: **Alan Wheatley**
Salt Lake City, Utah

Family Time

60

It is said that the family is the most important and most neglected of all values.

Are tasks from your highest-priority values making it to your Daily Task List?

Wayne and Judy Mills want to keep their priorities in order. Realizing there is no corporation in the world where the major executives do not meet regularly, and that the family is the most important organization, they determined, years ago, to meet as "executives." They meet one night each week, after the kids have gone to bed.

Judy explained that they used to discuss only that part of their week that was already planned for them, or their nondiscretionary time. Now that they have Franklin Planners, this is only the first item on the agenda. The second item is discretionary or free time, both individual and family. This includes progress toward mutual goals, family activities, and special needs of their four children. Their twelve-year-old daughter, Kierstin, also has a Planner. She and Judy plan her week and coordinate it with the family's plans. They also plan school assignments and deadlines. Then, they discuss the plans as a family, usually at the dinner table. Each child has the opportunity to participate in setting family goals and making plans.

Schedule time with each of your children, and with your spouse—for planning and playing.

Does it seem strange to set a weekly appointment with your spouse? If you wait until you're "free," your family may wait a long time. It's good to know there is a time set aside especially for them.

Source: **Wayne and Judy Mills**
Sandy, Utah

Blocking Time on the Monthly Calendar

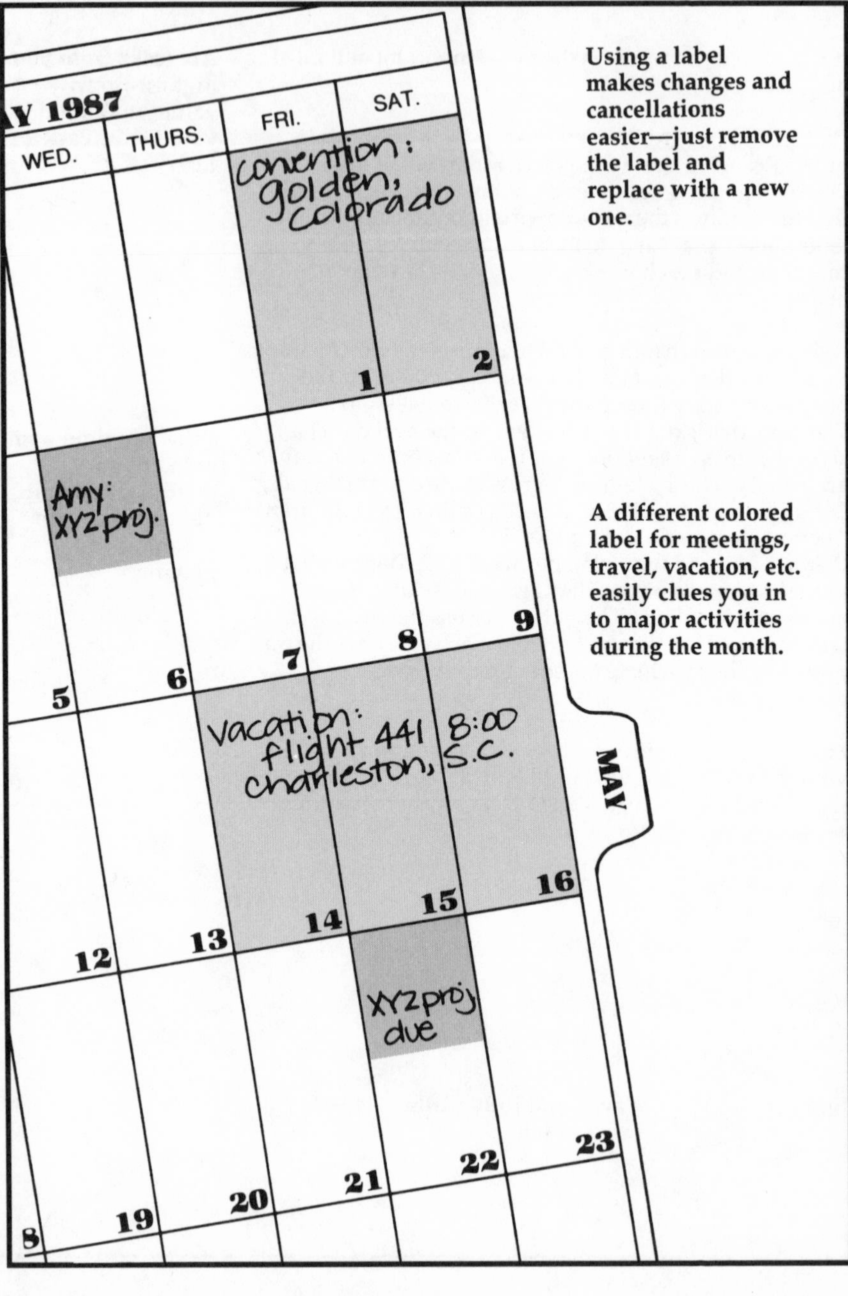

AY 1987
WED.
THURS.
FRI.
SAT.
convention: golden, colorado
1
2
Amy: XYZ proj.
5
6
7
8
9
vacation: flight 441 8:00 charleston, S.C.
12
13
14
15
16
XYZ proj. due
19
20
21
22
23
MAY
Using a label makes changes and cancellations easier—just remove the label and replace with a new one.
A different colored label for meetings, travel, vacation, etc. easily clues you in to major activities during the month.

When you know you will be traveling all day, or will be in a meeting from 9:00 to 3:00, it's easier to avoid double scheduling if there is a visual reminder that a large part of your day is already planned.

Jerry Pulsipher buys Avery labels that are 1/2" x 3/4"—half the size of the daily block on the Monthly Calendar. These come in all kinds of wild fluorescent colors that are sure to catch the eye of even the most forgetful. He uses one to block out a half day, or two for a full day. Green means he is traveling, orange means a special project to which he must devote himself. Being right-brained (more creative than logical), Jerry likes this kind of visual reminder.

But that doesn't mean that left-brained, logical people should ignore this idea. Dennis Webb is very left-brained and uses this technique also. He buys the larger sized label, as I mentioned in idea 37. His color scheme is a bit different, however. Red is for an all-day flight, orange is for long meetings, and yellow is for those days he is teaching. But the two most important colors for Dennis are blue and green. Blue is for days spent on the water—at Lake Powell or Lake Tahoe. And green is for those strenuous all-day golf games. If he wants to play only nine holes, he cuts the label in half with a Quick Clip, which covers only half the daily block on the Monthly Calendar.

There are definite advantages to this system (especially if you don't tell anyone what the green sticker means). For instance, when you use a highlighter pen for color blocking, pen ink often bleeds. On the labels it doesn't. If plans change, the label comes off; the Planner stays neat. And with all those colors on your Monthly Calendar, it makes your life look really exciting!

Ink won't bleed when written over labels.

Sources: **Jerry Pulsipher**
Dennis Webb
The Franklin Institute, Inc.
Salt Lake City, Utah

Scheduling Appointments for Another Person

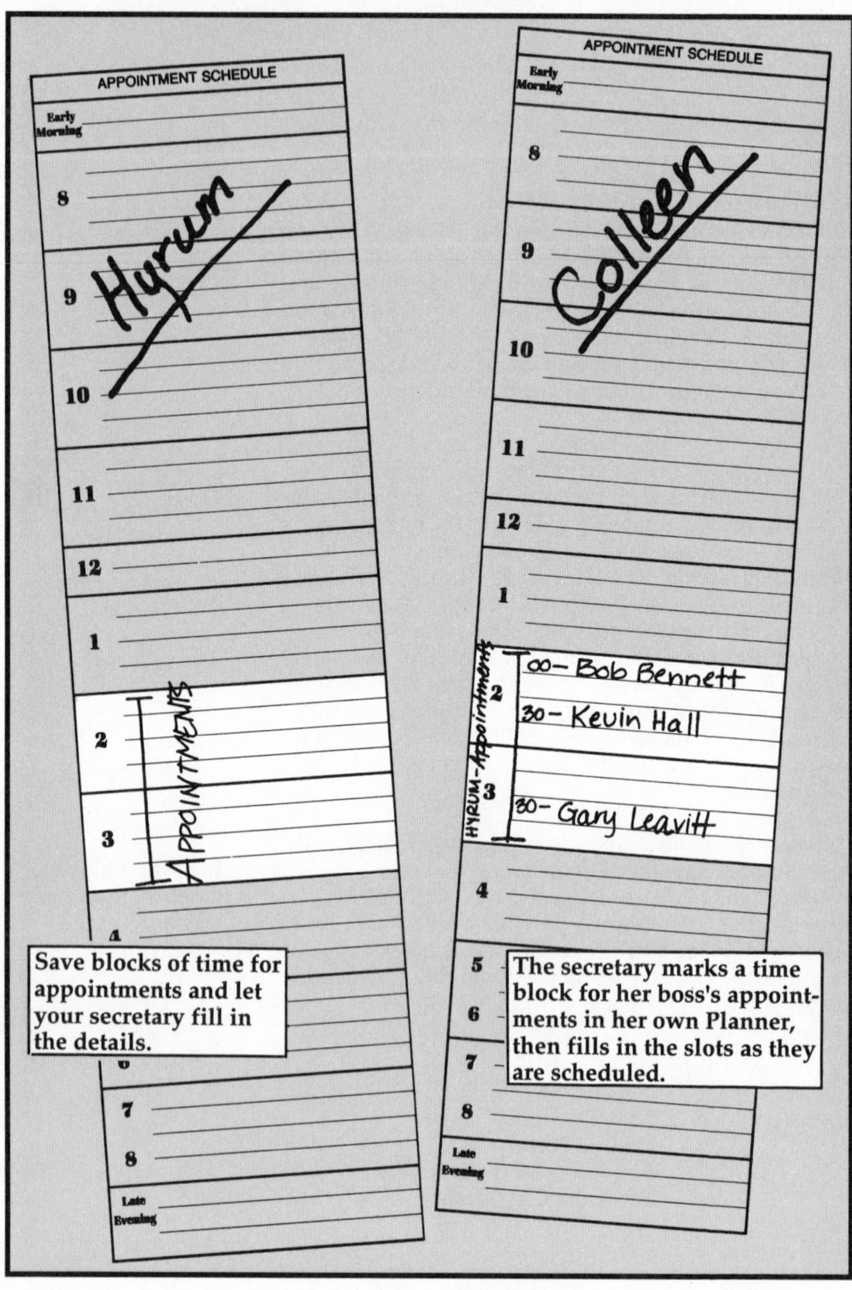

APPOINTMENT SCHEDULE
Early Morning
8
9
10
11
12
1
2
3
4
5
6
7
8
Late Evening
Hyrum
APPOINTMENTS
Save blocks of time for appointments and let your secretary fill in the details.
APPOINTMENT SCHEDULE
Early Morning
8
9
10
11
12
1
2
3
4
5
6
7
8
Late Evening
Colleen
HYRUM-Appointments
00- Bob Bennett
30- Kevin Hall
30- Gary Leavitt
The secretary marks a time block for her boss's appointments in her own Planner, then fills in the slots as they are scheduled.

62

In an office in New York City one morning while waiting for an appointment, I overheard the following conversation between an executive and his secretary:

"Good morning, Mr. B_______. Here are your messages from yesterday. You have two appointments today, one at 10:30 and one at 3:00."

"Appointments? I have no time for appointments today. You'll just have to cancel them."

"But last week you asked me to arrange appointments, and we agreed that today would be a good day."

"I'm sorry, Ruth. You'll just have to check with me before you make appointments."

With that he stormed into his office. Ruth turned to another secretary and said, "That's the third time this month. He's out of the office most of the time–how am I supposed to check with him for every appointment?"

Sitting in that lobby, I thought back to my own secretary (you guessed it), Colleen. We have a simple system that eliminates a lot of confusion. For the days that I am in town, I give to Colleen blocks of time for appointments. I set aside, for example, 2:00 to 4:00 p.m. and write "appointments" in the Appointment Schedule of my Day Planner. Colleen marks in her Planner "Hyrum appointments" in that block of time, then fills in the names as the meetings are arranged.

All you need to know is that this period of time is not available for anything else.

This saves us both some hassle—she doesn't have to wait until I am in the office to arrange meetings, and I can plan on those two hours devoted solely to appointments. If the appointment slots aren't filled—great! That's unexpected catch-up time.

Source: **Colleen Dom**
The Franklin Institute, Inc.
Salt Lake City, Utah

Reading Material

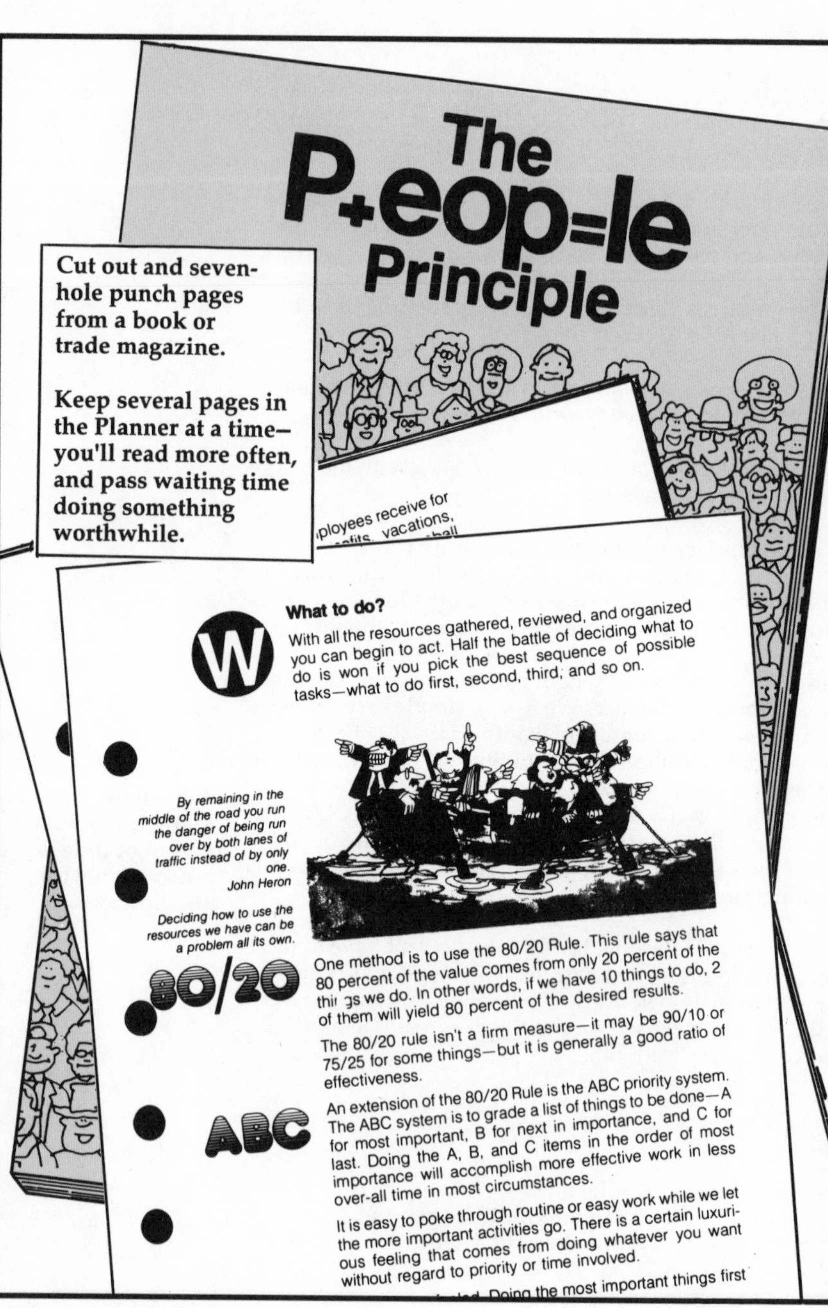

The P+eop=le Principle
Cut out and seven-hole punch pages from a book or trade magazine.
Keep several pages in the Planner at a time—you'll read more often, and pass waiting time doing something worthwhile.

What to do?

With all the resources gathered, reviewed, and organized you can begin to act. Half the battle of deciding what to do is won if you pick the best sequence of possible tasks—what to do first, second, third, and so on.

By remaining in the middle of the road you run the danger of being run over by both lanes of traffic instead of by only one.
John Heron

Deciding how to use the resources we have can be a problem all its own.

80/20

One method is to use the 80/20 Rule. This rule says that 80 percent of the value comes from only 20 percent of the things we do. In other words, if we have 10 things to do, 2 of them will yield 80 percent of the desired results.

The 80/20 rule isn't a firm measure—it may be 90/10 or 75/25 for some things—but it is generally a good ratio of effectiveness.

ABC

An extension of the 80/20 Rule is the ABC priority system. The ABC system is to grade a list of things to be done—A for most important, B for next in importance, and C for last. Doing the A, B, and C items in the order of most importance will accomplish more effective work in less over-all time in most circumstances.

It is easy to poke through routine or easy work while we let the more important activities go. There is a certain luxurious feeling that comes from doing whatever you want without regard to priority or time involved.

Doing the most important things first

While discussing values in a seminar once, I decided to ask how many of the participants thought they should do more reading. Every hand in the room went up. Then I asked them why they weren't doing it. There was a long pause. Finally, a hand went up in the back and the man said, "Books don't ring."

One of my values is to improve my mind, and I have made a list of books to read that will help me accomplish this. I buy these books in paperback, then cut out the pages and seven-hole punch them for my Franklin Day Planner. I keep several pages in the Planner at a time, so I always have something to read. I am now reading every day, whereas previously I read only occasionally. I am achieving greater inner peace because I am pursuing something which is very important to me. It is also something to do while waiting. So I kill two birds with one book!

Reading is rarely an urgency. Make time for it by making it more convenient.

The Three-Minute Memory Method

Each time the article surfaces in your Day Planner, take thirty seconds or so to scan the patterns you've identified. Then check off the appropriate box ("1dy" or "1mo," for example) and move the article ahead in your Planner to the next scheduled review.

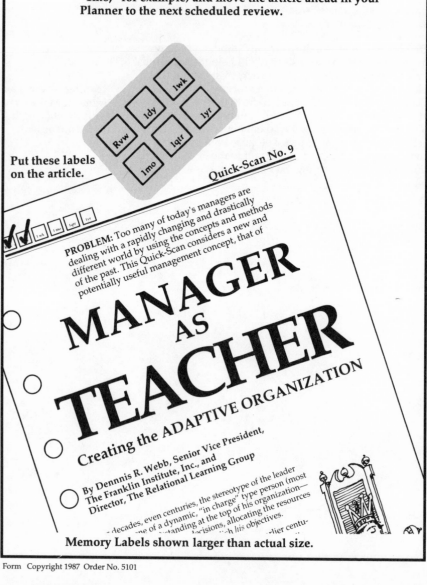

Put these labels on the article.

Quick-Scan No. 9
PROBLEM: Too many of today's managers are dealing with a rapidly changing and drastically different world by using the concepts and methods of the past. This Quick-Scan considers a new and potentially useful management concept, that of
MANAGER AS TEACHER
Creating the ADAPTIVE ORGANIZATION
By Dennis R. Webb, Senior Vice President, The Franklin Institute, Inc., and Director, The Relational Learning Group

Memory Labels shown larger than actual size.

Bob Bennett, CEO at Franklin, was telling an associate about our Three-Minute Memory Method. The man exclaimed, "I've been doing that for years—that's how I got through Harvard Law School."

This method was first published in an issue of *The Cutting Edge*, the Franklin Institute's productivity newsletter. The article outlines how your memory works and then presents a method for remembering based on this key concept:

> *By identifying an overall pattern to information and progressively reviewing the pattern at a rapid rate, you can shift the information from short-term memory to long-term memory.*

Want to remember the information you read? Try this simple method for keeping it in your long-term memory.

It's quite simple; there are three steps:

1. Read the material—articles, reports, anything that you want to store in long-term memory.

2. Review immediately—while the information is still fresh in your mind. Highlight key words or ideas. Let your mind naturally identify patterns and organize the material in a way that seems to fit. This may take as little as one minute.

3. Apply one of Franklin's Memory Labels to a corner of the article. Write today's date on the line above the boxes and check off the first box, "Rvw." Now place the article between tomorrow's pages in your Franklin Planner, where it will automatically come to your attention. Then scan the material regularly, following the schedule on the Memory Labels.

You'll be surprised at how much knowledge seeps in through such an effortless process. More information is available in the introductory issue of *The Cutting Edge*.

Source: **Bob Bennett**
The Franklin Institute, Inc.
Salt Lake City, Utah

Thirteen Column Spread Sheet

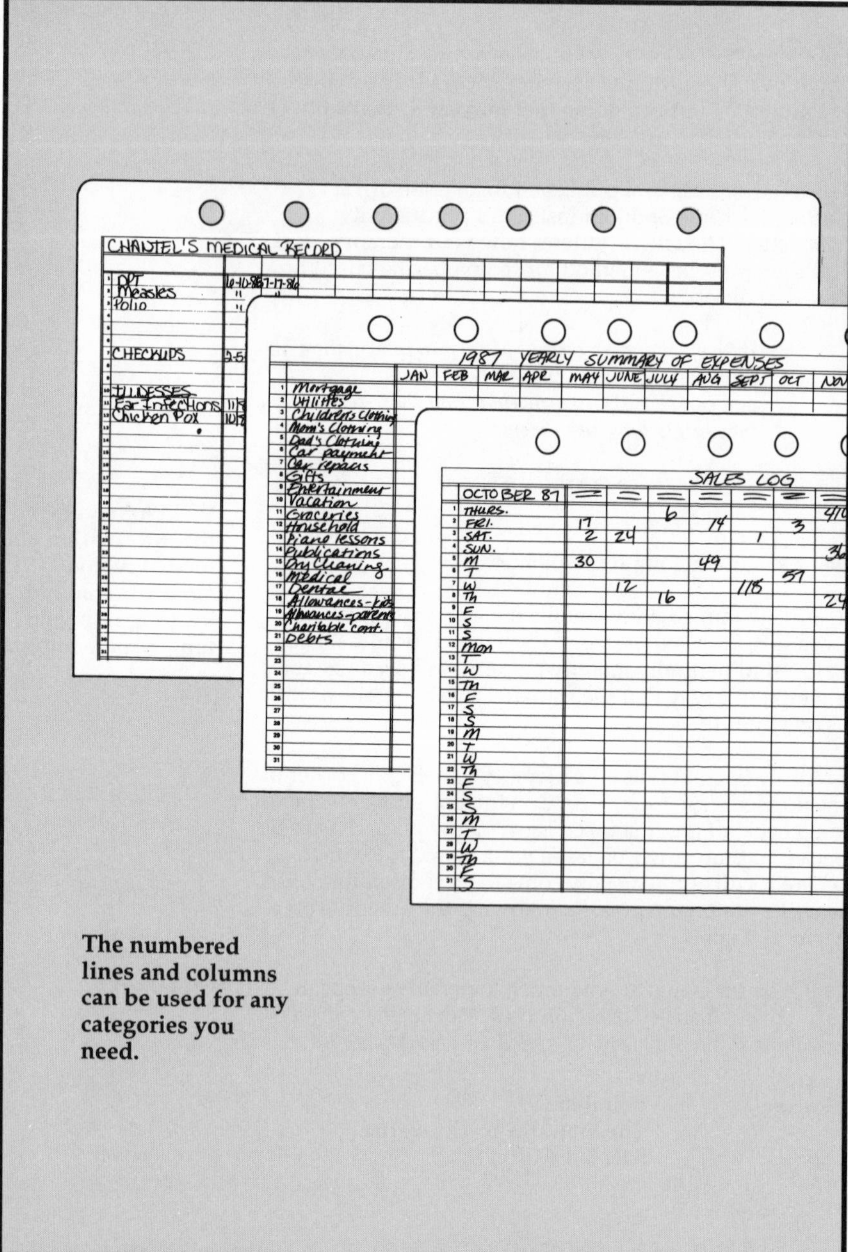

The numbered lines and columns can be used for any categories you need.

65

Have you ever noticed that most people have an innate fear of math? We usually avoid it, except to survive. Nobody plays calculus games at parties. And have you ever met anyone who loves balancing a checkbook?

I'll bet many people avoid the 13 Column Spread Sheet for the same reason: they think they are going to have to do some bookkeeping on it!

In reality, the 13 Column Spread Sheet is one of the most versatile forms available for the Day Planner. My wife uses one for each of our children's budgets. The columns are for the budget categories, and the numbered lines represent days of the month. This budget includes school expenses and extracurricular activities. Now that they know how much money they need each month, they ask for cost-of-living raises in allowance!

In previous Money Management seminars, we have encouraged that this sheet be used for a yearly summary of expenses. One month goes in each column, and budget items in the numbered lines. For the past year, record your monthly expenses in each of the budget categories. This will give a good overview of spending habits.

Salespeople like to use them as sales logs, using the numbered lines for the days of the month, and the columns for categories of items sold.

Karen Wilson keeps each of her children's medical records on a spread sheet. On the numbered lines she writes all required immunizations, checkups, diseases (mumps, measles, etc.). She records dates in the columns.

The nice thing about this form is that it is adaptable to any situation.

Sources: **Gail Smith**
Karen Wilson
The Franklin Institute, Inc.
Salt Lake City, Utah

Day Finder

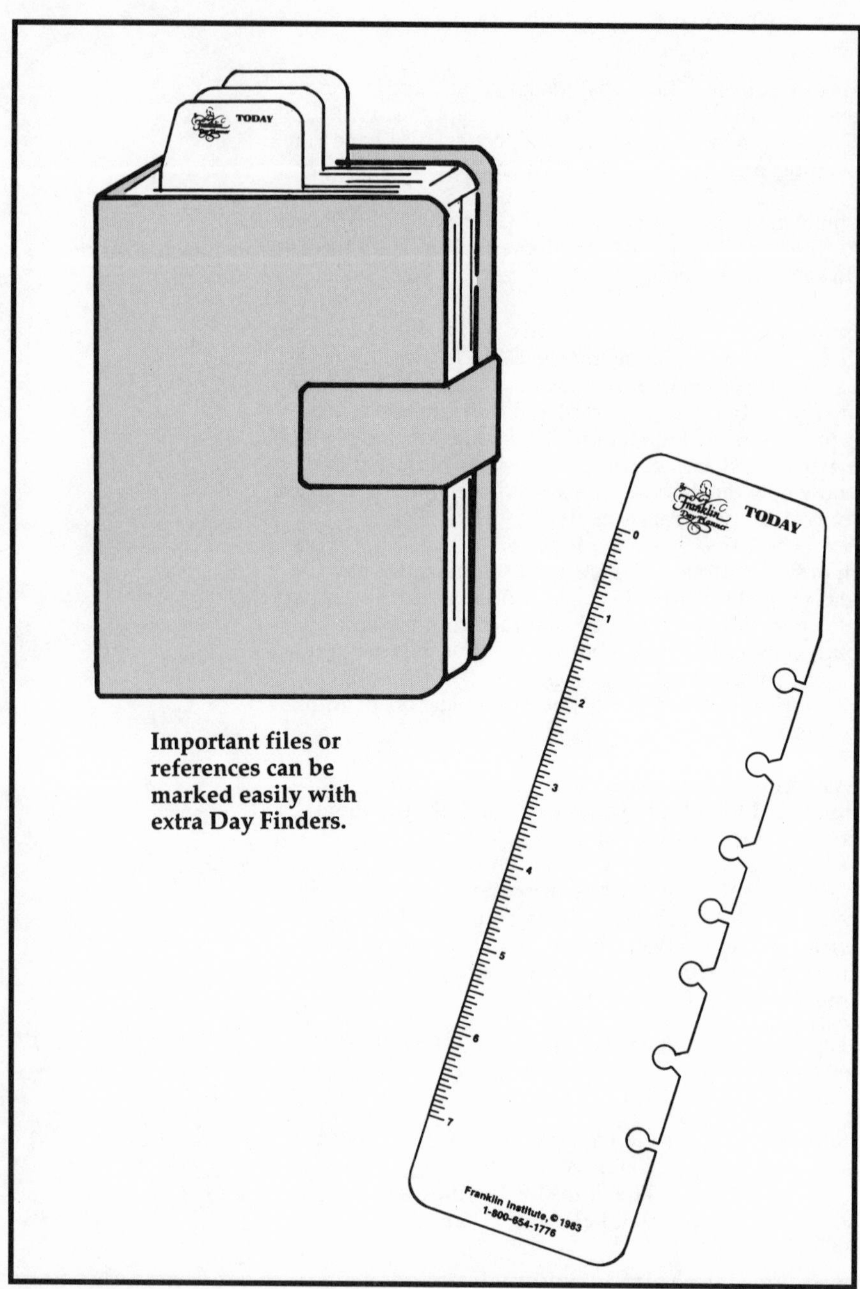

Important files or references can be marked easily with extra Day Finders.

Order No. 4011

On our way to Hawaii not too long ago, my wife and I sat by a man with the thickest Franklin Day Planner I have ever seen. He really keeps his whole life in there. I asked him if he ever loses track of the information he keeps in the Planner. But as I spoke, I noticed about ten Day Finders sticking out of the top and bottom of the Planner. He had each Day Finder labeled with the file it marked. When he cannot remember where something is, he simply reads his Day Finders!

Ten may be overdoing it. But many people keep a few extras to mark files frequently referred to. Tom Young keeps several Day Finders to mark project files, Christmas lists, meeting plans, and a Check Register page for quick access.

Be creative—an extra Day Finder could come in handy more often than you think.

The Day Finder is designed as a ruler also. Anytime you need a measurement or a straight line, you need only go as far as your Planner—and where is your Day Planner always?

If you don't have a Seven-Hole Punch yet, and need to punch a page or two to fit in your Planner, the Day Finder makes a good marking guide for the hole pattern.

There are myriad other ways to use them. Our toll-free number is printed at the bottom of your Day Finder if you'd like to know what they are!

Source: **Tom Young**
Young Electric Sign Co.
Salt Lake City, Utah

Yearly Calendar

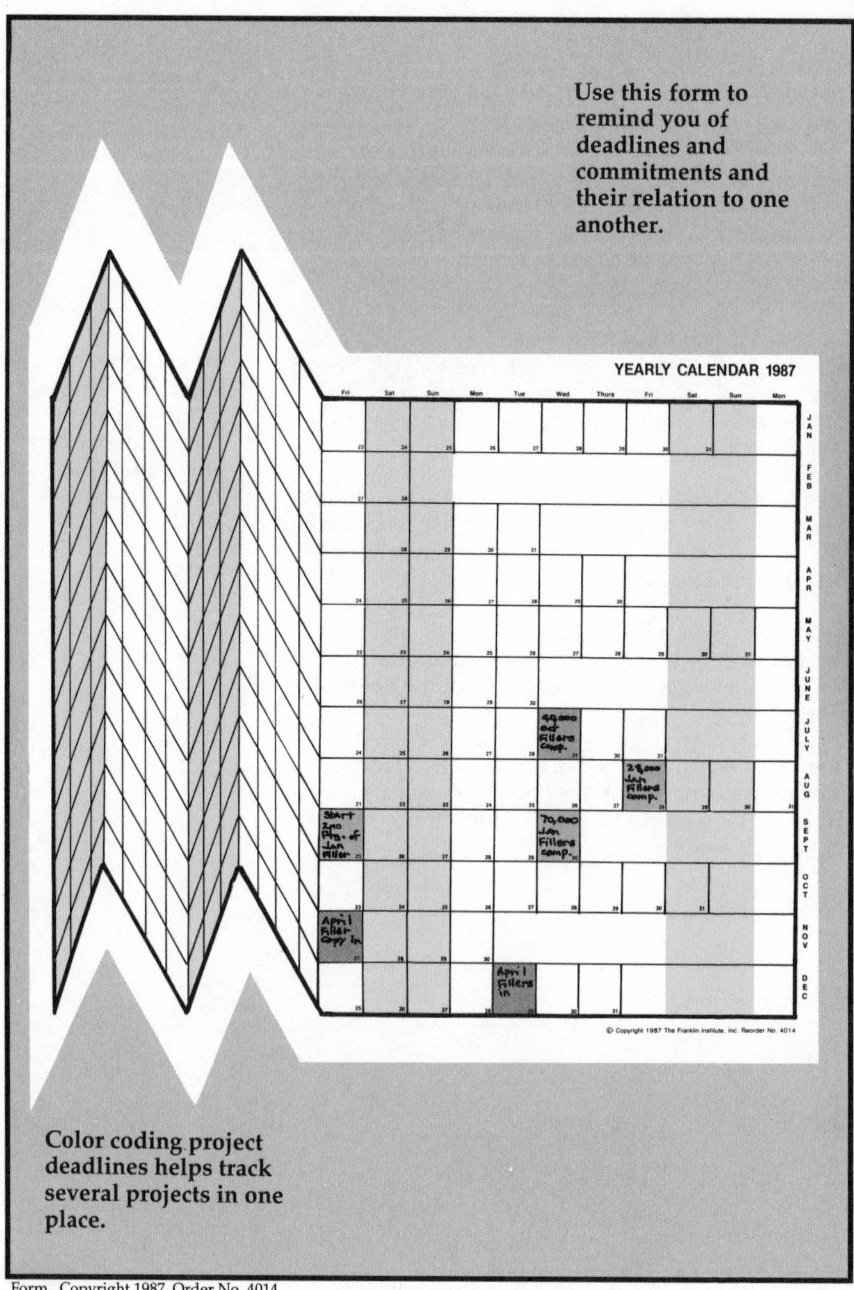

Form Copyright 1987 Order No. 4014

Some businesses cannot survive long if they miss deadlines. Garff Cannon owns the bindery that prints the Franklin Planners. If he could not meet our printing deadlines, we would take our business elsewhere.

Use the Yearly Calendar form to remind you of deadlines and commitments and their relation to one another.

He uses the Yearly Calendar form to visualize all deadlines in relation to one another. This form spreads out to show each day of the year. Garff has four major deadlines per year: the January, April, July, and October fillers. For each of these, there are several components with individual deadlines, and they all overlap. Therefore, he designates each of the four major projects by color.

For example, the January filler deadlines are highlighted in blue. Each project contributing to completion of the January filler has its own deadline, and is highlighted in blue. April filler deadlines are yellow, July's are orange, and October's are green. As projects overlap, there is no confusion about which main deadline they relate to.

At a glance, he can see what's going on. No deadlines "sneak up" on him. He is more in control because he sees daily the direction he is going.

Source: **Garff Cannon**
Richmarc, Inc.
Salt Lake City, Utah

Corporate Goals

1 **Include managers and department heads in the creation of a company mission statement.**

2 **Each department meets together and discusses how it can contribute.**

3 **Employees determine ways in which they will contribute to the fulfillment of the Company Mission.**

At Wallace Associates, every employee is aware of and involved in the accomplishment of company-wide goals. Individually and departmentally they are working toward achieving the standards set forth in the Company Mission Statement.

After the officers and managers in the company define a mission statement, each department meets to discuss how they can contribute to the company's success, keeping the mission statement foremost in their minds. Progress on these goals is evaluated regularly in departmental meetings.

Individuals also set goals to contribute to the organization's success. There are three questions that each employee answers during this goal-setting process: (1) How can I contribute to the success of Wallace Associates on a company-wide basis? What can I do that will benefit the whole organization?, (2) What can I do within my job tasks that will help Wallace Associates achieve its goals? and, (3) What can I do personally to contribute to my own and the organization's success?

One employee of Wallace Associates explained to me how she would answer these questions. She determined that installing a new software system will benefit the company and further its progress toward defined goals. Testing the new software is a way that progress will be enhanced through her job tasks. And she can contribute personally by further educating herself about software packages and systems.

Through a deliberate goal-setting effort, each employee is offering a significant contribution to the company good.

Source: **Wallace Associates Companies**
Salt Lake City, Utah

Daily Expense Section

Beginning balance goes here.

DAILY EXPENSES

Begin Balance - 2800-
Subway 140
Add ¥14,000 Lunch 5400
Subway 140
Spent- ¥5680
total Fwd- 11120

DAILY EXPENSES

Begin Bal- ¥10,000 Cab 530
Lunch 2100
Paper 100
Subway 140
Spent - total. ¥2870
total Fwd- 7130

DAILY EXPENSES

Begin. Bal. ¥7130 Cab 670
Cab 1010
Lunch 2300
Magazine 350
Spent- total ¥4330
total Fwd- 2800

Record the day's expenses, then figure the ending balance for the day.

I'll let Bob Bennett tell you about his idea.

> *I often travel abroad, and deal with different currencies. On one trip to Japan, I decided to keep meticulous track of how the money was spent. I put a "beginning balance" under Daily Expenses on the left-hand side of my Day Planner—the total amount of yen I had. During the day, I wrote specific expenses in that section.*
>
> *Sometimes, I forgot to jot down a cab fare or tip paid in a hurry. However, with the beginning balance written in my Planner, I was able to count my money in the hotel room each night and determine how much cash had been handed out but not recorded. Since I reviewed daily, it was usually easy to remember where that extra 5,000 yen had gone. One day's ending balance became the next day's beginning balance, as I moved from page to page.*
>
> *Using the Daily Expenses section this way has vastly increased my control over spending habits, both at home and abroad, as well as my confidence about defending my expense account to the IRS.*

Source: **Bob Bennett**
The Franklin Institute, Inc.
Salt Lake City, Utah

More on Correcting the Monthly Calendar

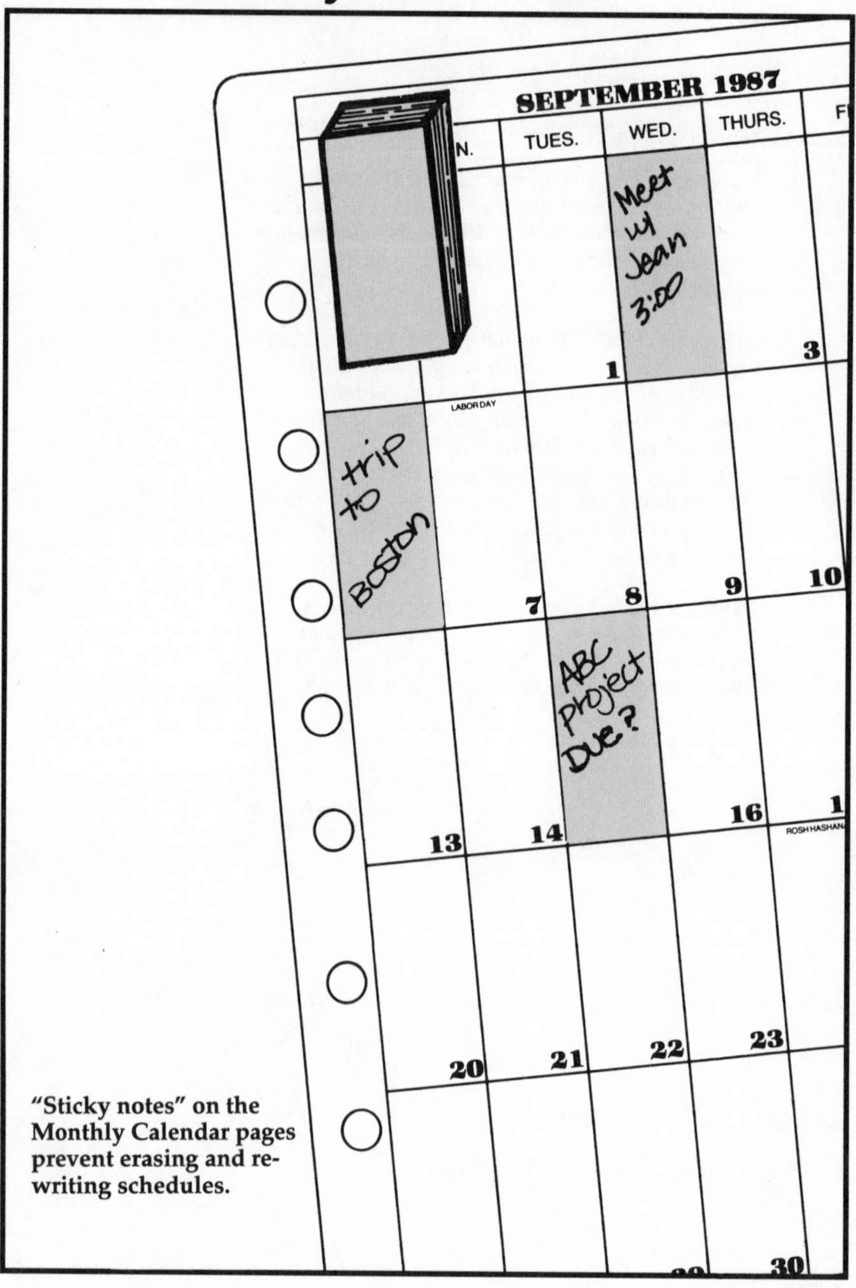

"Sticky notes" on the Monthly Calendar pages prevent erasing and re-writing schedules.

70

This idea comes from a Dow Chemical employee in Canada. Kurt Hanks, from our Research and Development Department, met him on a recent trip.

I was on a flight from New York to Ontario and met a man from Mississauga, Ontario. We had a pleasant conversation about how to spell and pronounce Mississauga. I asked him to write it down for me, and he pulled out a Franklin Planner to get a piece of paper. He was excited to learn that I work for Franklin and he spent the next hour and a half explaining all the "custom designs" he had devised for it. He said he spent fifteen percent of his time in the first six months developing these little tricks. Here's one of them.

He buys yellow sticky note pads by the dozens and cuts them in thirds. Each section fits very nicely over a day's block on the Monthly Calendar. When a meeting or event is scheduled for a future month, he writes it on the yellow paper instead of right on the Monthly Calendar. If the date is changed, all he has to do is stick the note on a different day. He keeps a supply of these sticky notes at the top corner of each Monthly Calendar page; no matter which month he is planning, he has a supply of the sticky notes at hand.

Source: **Claude Mongrain**
Dow Chemical Canada
Mississauga, Ontario

Learning Vocabulary

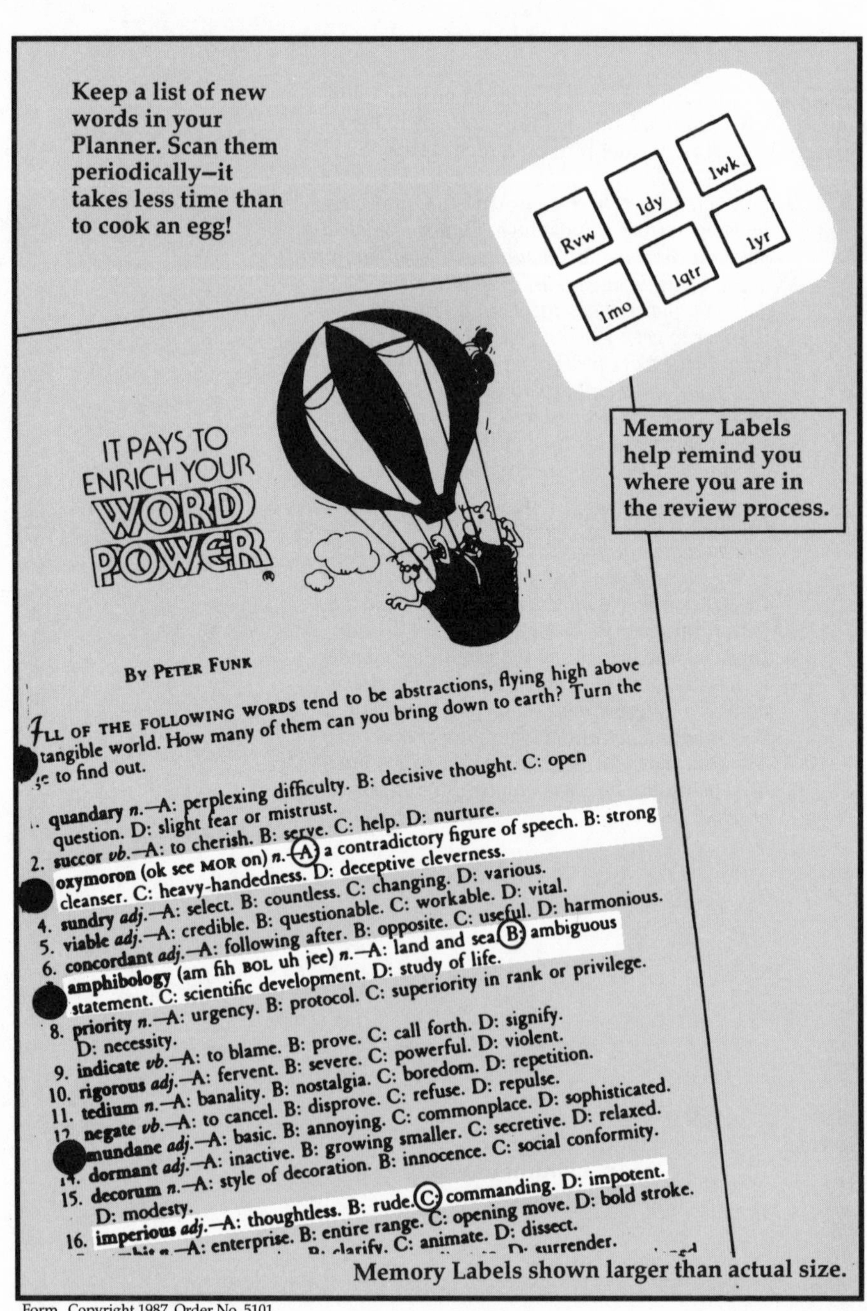

Keep a list of new words in your Planner. Scan them periodically–it takes less time than to cook an egg!
Rvw
1dy
1wk
1mo
1qtr
1yr
Memory Labels help remind you where you are in the review process.
IT PAYS TO ENRICH YOUR WORD POWER®

BY PETER FUNK

ALL OF THE FOLLOWING WORDS tend to be abstractions, flying high above tangible world. How many of them can you bring down to earth? Turn the ge to find out.

1. **quandary** *n.*—A: perplexing difficulty. B: decisive thought. C: open question. D: slight fear or mistrust.
2. **succor** *vb.*—A: to cherish. B: serve. C: help. D: nurture.
oxymoron (ok see MOR on) *n.*—Ⓐ a contradictory figure of speech. B: strong cleanser. C: heavy-handedness. D: deceptive cleverness.
4. **sundry** *adj.*—A: select. B: countless. C: changing. D: various.
5. **viable** *adj.*—A: credible. B: questionable. C: workable. D: vital.
6. **concordant** *adj.*—A: following after. B: opposite. C: useful. D: harmonious.
amphibology (am fih BOL uh jee) *n.*—A: land and sea. Ⓑ ambiguous statement. C: scientific development. D: study of life.
8. **priority** *n.*—A: urgency. B: protocol. C: superiority in rank or privilege. D: necessity.
9. **indicate** *vb.*—A: to blame. B: prove. C: call forth. D: signify.
10. **rigorous** *adj.*—A: fervent. B: severe. C: powerful. D: violent.
11. **tedium** *n.*—A: banality. B: nostalgia. C: boredom. D: repetition.
12. **negate** *vb.*—A: to cancel. B: disprove. C: refuse. D: repulse.
mundane *adj.*—A: basic. B: annoying. C: commonplace. D: sophisticated.
14. **dormant** *adj.*—A: inactive. B: growing smaller. C: secretive. D: relaxed.
15. **decorum** *n.*—A: style of decoration. B: innocence. C: social conformity. D: modesty.
16. **imperious** *adj.*—A: thoughtless. B: rude. Ⓒ commanding. D: impotent.
...bit *n.*—A: enterprise. B: entire range. C: opening move. D: bold stroke.
... B: clarify. C: animate. D: dissect.
... D: surrender.

Memory Labels shown larger than actual size.

71

Words are the tools of thought. Margaret Broadley said in her book *Your Natural Gifts*, "Low vocabulary decreases the effectiveness of inborn gifts in any civilization." Clearly, a strong vocabulary enables people to be more successful because they are better able to express themselves and understand others.

Lynn Robbins, recognizing the benefits of a large vocabulary, keeps a vocabulary list (from *Reader's Digest*) in his Planner. He applies the Three-Minute Memory Method to those words he needs to learn.

Three-Minute Memory Method

The day Lynn reads the list, he highlights in yellow those words he wants to learn, then places the list in between the following day's pages of the Planner. The next day he takes no more than a few seconds to review the highlighted words and their definitions. Then he moves the page to the next review date, one week later. After review, he moves it ahead, first one month, then one quarter, then one year down the road. These quick periodic reviews make all the difference.

The Memory Labels, explained in idea 64, are tools to help you remember where you are in the review process. Lynn has had very good results using this method for learning vocabulary. And, of course, the Three-Minute Memory Method can be applied to any piece of information you want to remember.

Source: **Lynn Robbins**
The Franklin Institute, Inc.
Salt Lake City, Utah

Coding Phone Calls

28
SUNDAY
JUNE 28
1987

S	M	T	W	T	F	S
	1	2	3	4	5	6
7	8	9	10	11	12	13
14	15	16	17	18	19	20
21	22	23	24	25	26	27
28	29	30				

179th Day
186 Left

✓ = Task Completed
→ = Planned Forward
× = Task Deleted
G⊘ = Delegated Task
• = In Process

↓	ABC PRIORITY	PRIORITIZED DAILY TASK LIST
	P	Mark Anderson
	P	Jody re meeting
	P	Becky Haymond
	B2	Harold Brock back-appt. •
	B4	Phil - Board Meeting •
	C3	Price on new desk •

APPOINTM[ENTS]

Early Morning
8
9
10
11
12
1
2
3
4

Distinguish phoning tasks with a special code so you can find them quickly in a long Daily Task List.

Your Daily Task List is usually long. Somewhere in that list, there are several phone calls to make. You have twenty minutes and would like to get them all done at once. But it is frustrating to read the list over and over to find each call. Why not simplify the process by adding a special code just for phone calls?

That is what Marlene Anderson does. She makes several phone calls per day, and can often accomplish another task on her list at the same time. She added the code "P" for phone calls. This way, the day's calls stand apart from the rest of the tasks.

Scott Doscher suggests putting a dot by everything that can be accomplished over the phone. Since he isn't by a phone all day long, this helps him get all calling done at one time.

Make all calls at one time.

Making all your phone calls at once is a good way to increase productivity. It frees up more time for other activities. These suggestions make that phoning time even more productive.

Sources:

Marlene Anderson
Riverside, California

Scott Doscher
Salt Lake City, Utah

Goal Reminder on a Day Finder

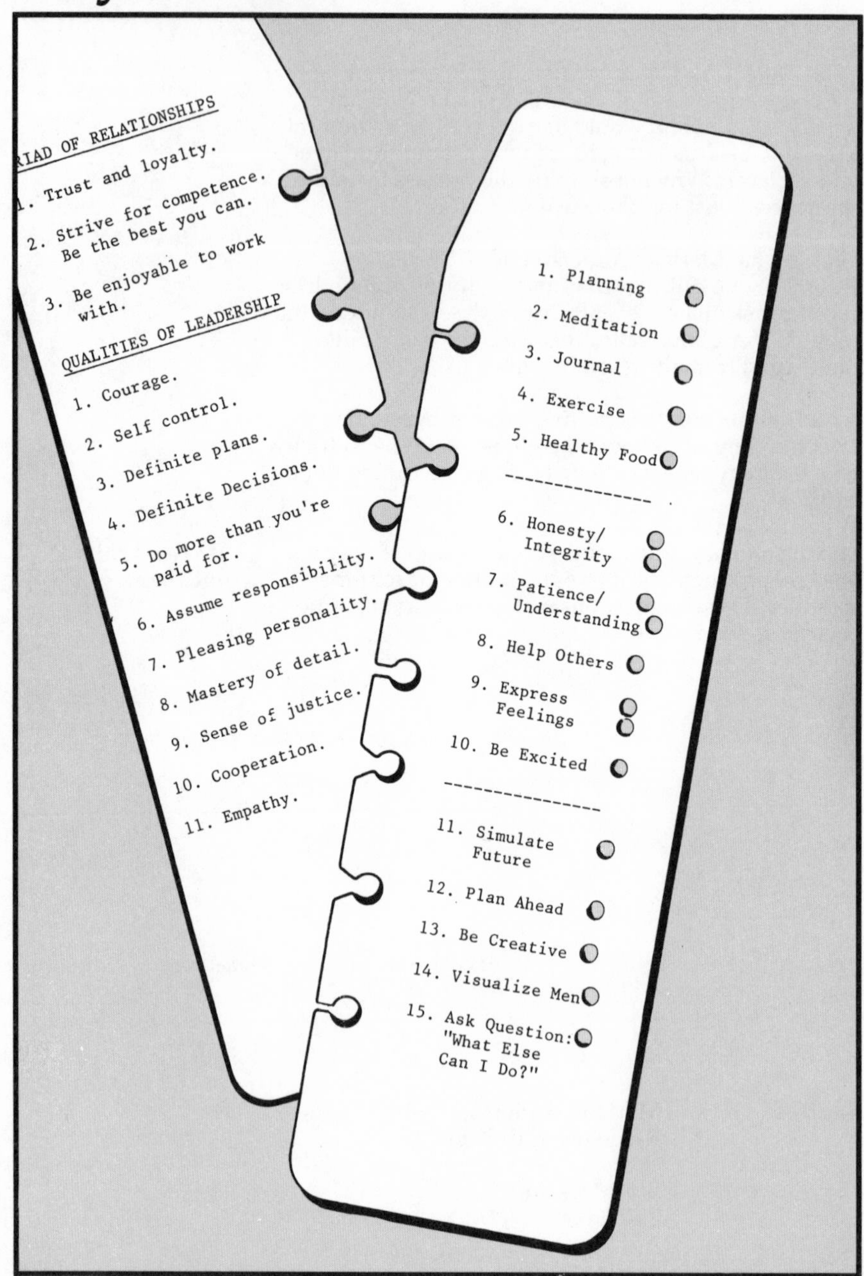

RIAD OF RELATIONSHIPS
1. Trust and loyalty.
2. Strive for competence. Be the best you can.
3. Be enjoyable to work with.
QUALITIES OF LEADERSHIP
1. Courage.
2. Self control.
3. Definite plans.
4. Definite Decisions.
5. Do more than you're paid for.
6. Assume responsibility.
7. Pleasing personality.
8. Mastery of detail.
9. Sense of justice.
10. Cooperation.
11. Empathy.
1. Planning
2. Meditation
3. Journal
4. Exercise
5. Healthy Food
6. Honesty/ Integrity
7. Patience/ Understanding
8. Help Others
9. Express Feelings
10. Be Excited
11. Simulate Future
12. Plan Ahead
13. Be Creative
14. Visualize Men
15. Ask Question: "What Else Can I Do?"

Day Finder Copyright 1987 Order No.4011

73

The old maxim "out of sight, out of mind" can apply to more than girlfriends or boyfriends. What about goals, for example. Do you remember each of your Governing Values? Do daily tasks aimed at achieving those goals regularly appear in your Daily Task Lists?

Dave Williams is a very goal-oriented person. He likes having his goals right in front of him because it helps him keep focused. So he has a special Day Finder made with what he calls his "Daily Essentials" printed on it. These are things he wants to work toward every day in order to be happy. To the right of each item is a cut-out hole through which he checks off these tasks. Because the goals are always where he can see them, he works on them more consistently.

As sales manager for a corporation, he printed goal reminders and the company logo on two hundred Day Finders for his associates. (The Franklin Institute will print special Day Finders with company logos.) Each salesperson was reminded daily of the qualities of leadership that would help him or her be more successful in the organization and in life.

This kind of daily reminder can make a big difference in achieving your goals. It's like the dangling carrot approach—you work harder to reach it because you can see it's just in front of you. With each daily task accomplished, you get closer and closer to the "carrot."

Source: **Dave Williams**
Lethbridge, Alberta, Canada

Scheduling for Several People

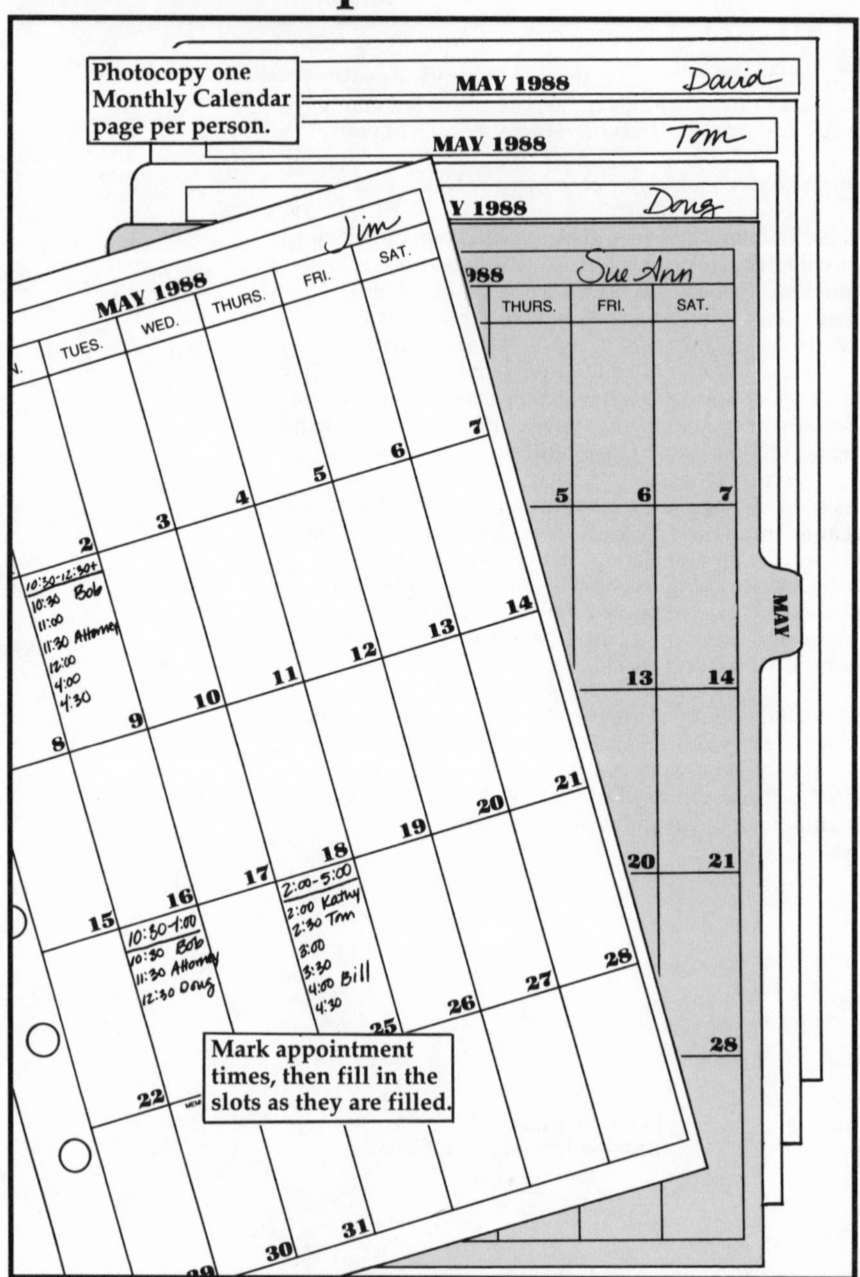

74

In idea 62, I explained a method of scheduling appointments for one other person. Sometimes, one secretary is scheduling for four or five people.

Sue Ann Whittier is an executive secretary and schedules appointments for four vice presidents. Each of them travels a lot, and spends many hours in appointments every week. In order to juggle the appointments, she makes four photocopies of every Monthly Calendar page. The tabbed page is her own. The other four are for each of her bosses.

On Monday mornings, Sue Ann checks with Jim, Doug, David, and Tom to get open times for appointments. On the Monthly Calendar page for Jim, she notes that there is time between 10:30 and 1:00 on Tuesday for appointments. That afternoon, a director in the company asks if Jim has time to see him Tuesday. Sue Ann schedules him at 10:30. Later, the attorney calls to set up an appointment with Jim and asks when he is free; Sue Ann schedules him at 11:30. Tuesday morning, when Jim comes in the office, Sue Ann informs him of his appointments. After the attorney leaves at 12:15, Jim has forty-five minutes to finish the project he was working on earlier.

Sue Ann said, "This technique has saved my sanity. I used to be a bumbling fool, shuffling papers and looking like a scatterbrain. Now that I am using Monthly Calendar pages for appointments, we all can't believe how smoothly the office is running."

Source: **Sue Ann Whittier**
Sacramento, California

Money Management For Children

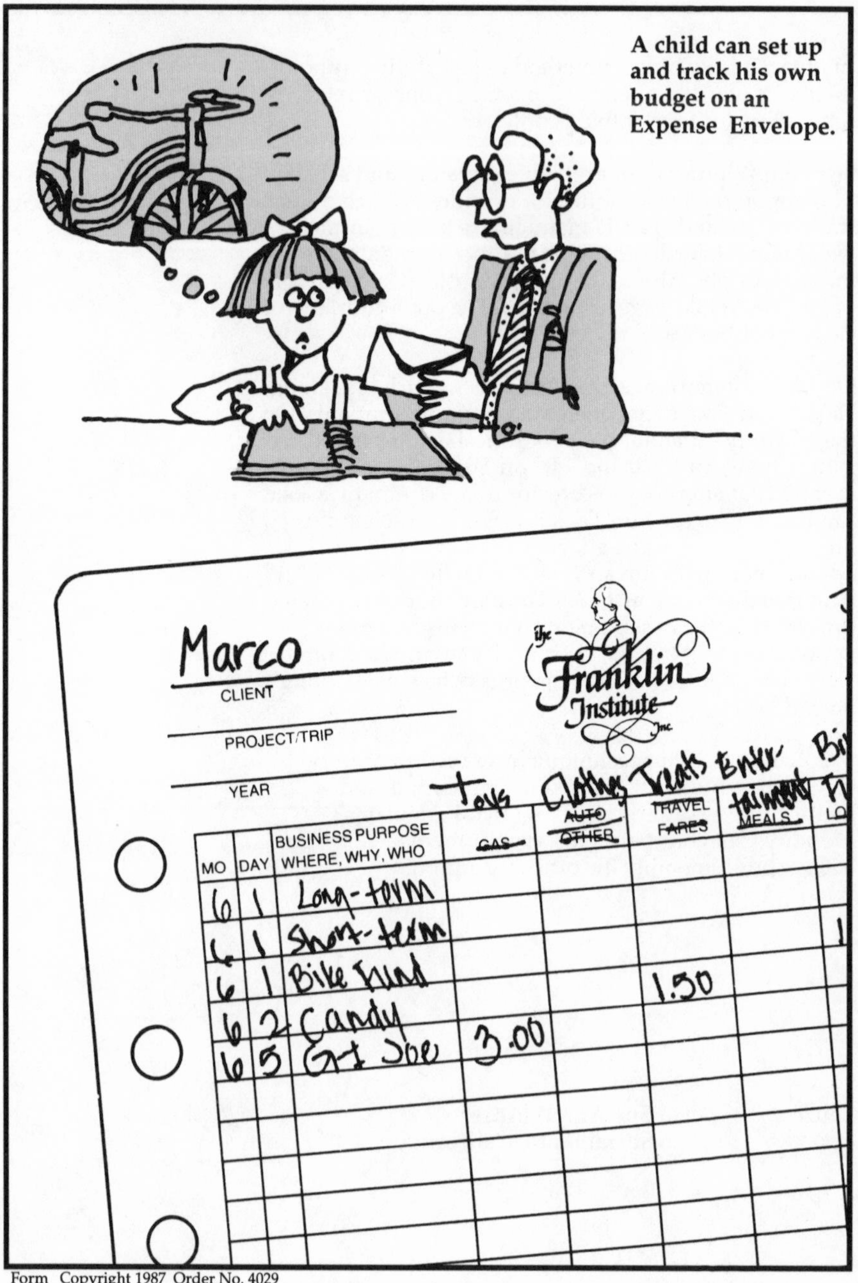

A child can set up and track his own budget on an Expense Envelope.

When Garff and Kim Cannon hired their kids to work in their bindery Saturdays, they decided to pay them regular wages. "That way," they thought, "we won't have to worry about allowances and entertainment money for the kids this summer." Garff now comments sadly, "They made a lot of money for kids their age, and what have they got to show for it? Nothing."

This year, they are prepared—they have devised a tool for teaching their children some financial responsibility.

First, provide a little guidance by having a monthly Money Meeting.

First, they meet with each child individually—the kids call these "Money Meetings." They set a budget, including savings for college and major purchases (bicycle, baseball mitt, stereo). At the beginning of each month, the kids get an Expense Envelope with their paycheck (if working) or allowance in it.

Across the seven columns on the front, each child writes his or her budget categories and amounts. Every time Richard, for example, makes a purchase, he writes what he bought and records the amount under the corresponding budget category. He knows that he won't get any more money during the month, so he is careful to not spend it all the first week.

Richard thinks twice now about how he spends his money, because he knows he will have to report it all to his dad. At the end of the month, Richard and Garff have another Money Meeting. They review what he spent his money on, whether he met his savings goals, and they set new goals for the coming month.

The Cannons are pleased with the progress their children are making towards being financially responsible. And the kids are happy, too, with their new bikes and dolls and mitts.

Sources: **Garff and Kim Cannon**
Richard, Marco, Geoffrey, Kathryn
Richmarc Bindery
Salt Lake City, Utah

Birthday List

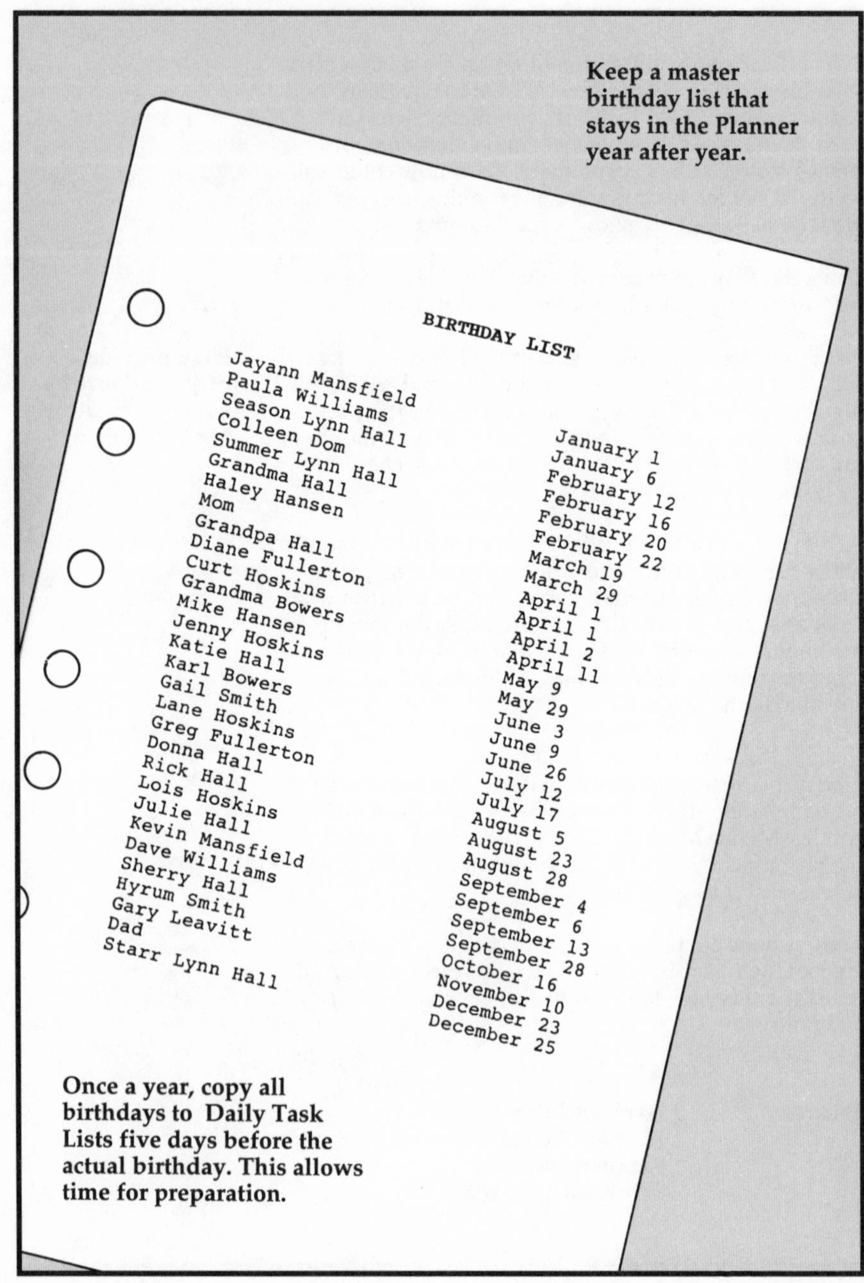

Keep a master birthday list that stays in the Planner year after year.

BIRTHDAY LIST

Jayann Mansfield	January 1
Paula Williams	January 6
Season Lynn Hall	February 12
Colleen Dom	February 16
Summer Lynn Hall	February 20
Grandma Hall	February 22
Haley Hansen	March 19
Mom	March 29
Grandpa Hall	April 1
Diane Fullerton	April 1
Curt Hoskins	April 2
Grandma Bowers	April 11
Mike Hansen	May 9
Jenny Hoskins	May 29
Katie Hall	June 3
Karl Bowers	June 9
Gail Smith	June 26
Lane Hoskins	July 12
Greg Fullerton	July 17
Donna Hall	August 5
Rick Hall	August 23
Lois Hoskins	August 28
Julie Hall	September 4
Kevin Mansfield	September 6
Dave Williams	September 13
Sherry Hall	September 28
Hyrum Smith	October 16
Gary Leavitt	November 10
Dad	December 23
Starr Lynn Hall	December 25

Once a year, copy all birthdays to Daily Task Lists five days before the actual birthday. This allows time for preparation.

76

Remembering birthdays is one of life's great challenges. If you have ever forgotten your spouse's birthday, you know what I mean.

We have had so many requests for a birthday list in the Planner that the 1988 refill will include one in the Key Information section.

Kevin Hall has realized that it doesn't do him much good to remember his wife's birthday ON her birthday; by then it's too late to find out what she wants and to make plans. And she knows by that time that he has forgotten, even if he does come home with flowers and candy.

So Kevin developed a foolproof system for remembering birthdays. He keeps a birthday list in the Key Information section. At the beginning of each new year, he goes to his Storage Binder and writes in the birthdays on the Daily Task List *five days before* the actual birthday. This is the key. When he opens the Planner on the morning of September 23rd and it says "Sherry (9-28)," he knows he has five days to prepare for her birthday.

Write the reminder on the Daily Task List to remind you to TAKE ACTION!

He likes this method because he has to fill in birthdays only once a year, and because it puts a reminder in a place of action—the Daily Task List. And that reminds him that if he doesn't take action, he's in big trouble.

Source: **Kevin Hall**
The Franklin Institute, Inc.
Salt Lake City, Utah

Survival Kits

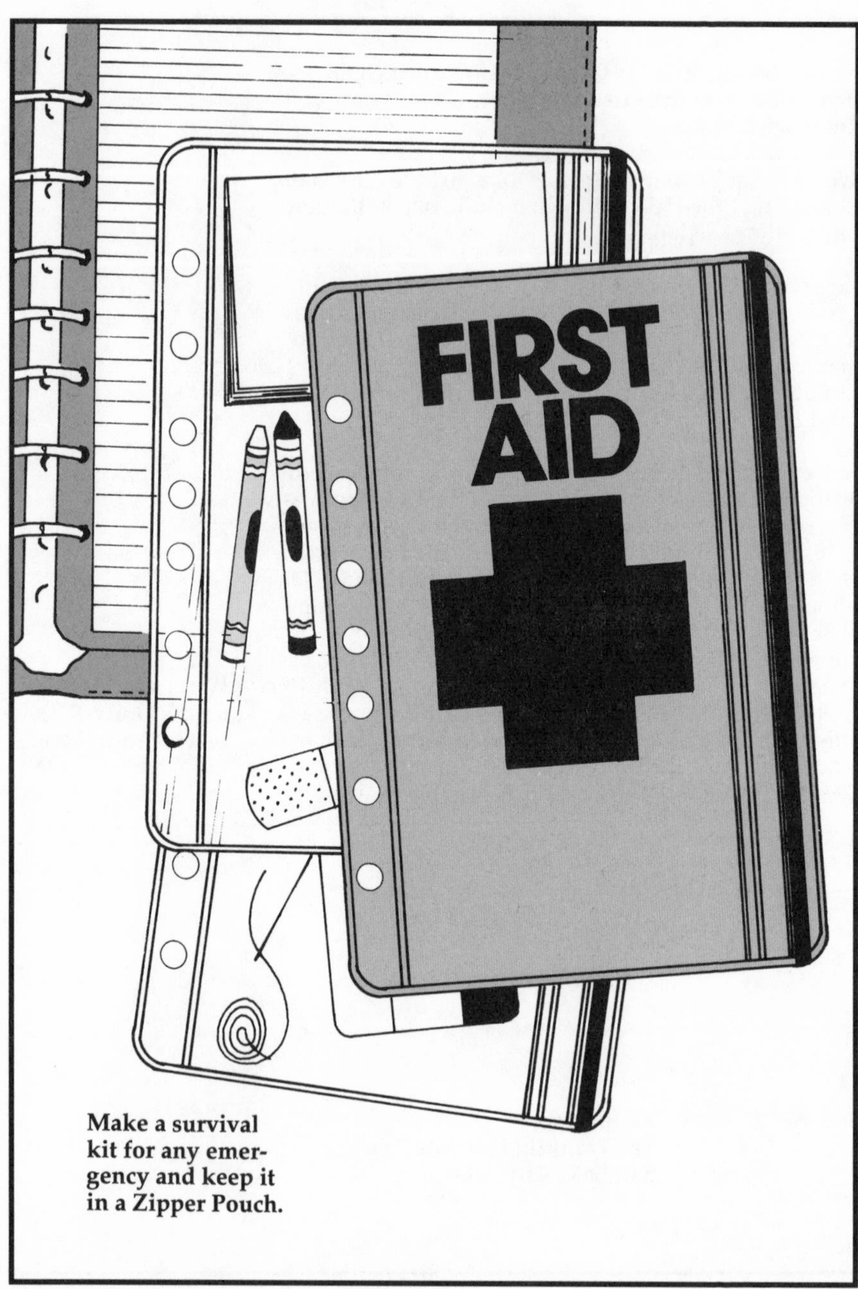

Make a survival kit for any emergency and keep it in a Zipper Pouch.

Zipper Pouch Order No. 4008

Martha Wallace could not find a babysitter, and so had to take her three-year-old, Jason, to her PTA meeting. Despite the fact that Martha brought toys for him, Jason disrupted the whole meeting. He was hungry. He wanted a different toy. He fell and scraped his elbow. By the time they got home, Martha was exhausted.

Joseph Sturzman wasn't having a great day either. At his 10:00 meeting with a client, a button popped off his shirt. And his Cross pen ran out of ink. At lunch, he spilled on his new silk tie. He went to pay the tab, and remembered that his wife had borrowed his credit card.

Martha and Joseph were in bad need of preparation for emergencies; being prepared makes those "bad days" a little more bearable.

Martha made herself a "Jason Survival Kit" for those times she needs to take Jason somewhere where he may be bored. The kit includes Band-Aids, raisins and Cheerios, blank paper, crayons, and wet wipes; she keeps all this in a Zipper Pouch. She still brings toys for him and uses the Survival Kit only in an emergency: a long shopping trip, or a day when Jason isn't feeling well.

Put your Survival Kit in a Zipper Pouch.

Joseph now carries an Executive Survival Kit. A needle and thread, pen refill, nail file, emergency-only credit card, and Kleenex have spared him many headaches. Because a tie will get rumpled in a Zipper Pouch, keep a spare at the office—always. This little trick has saved me several times.

You can make a Zipper Pouch Survival Kit for every possible emergency: work, travel, first aid, children, or whatever. They are portable and interchangeable. Keep them all in one place (a Storage Binder, perhaps) and take with you only the one you need.

Sources: **Martha Wallace**
Boise, Idaho

Joseph Sturzman
New York City, New York

Poems and Quotations

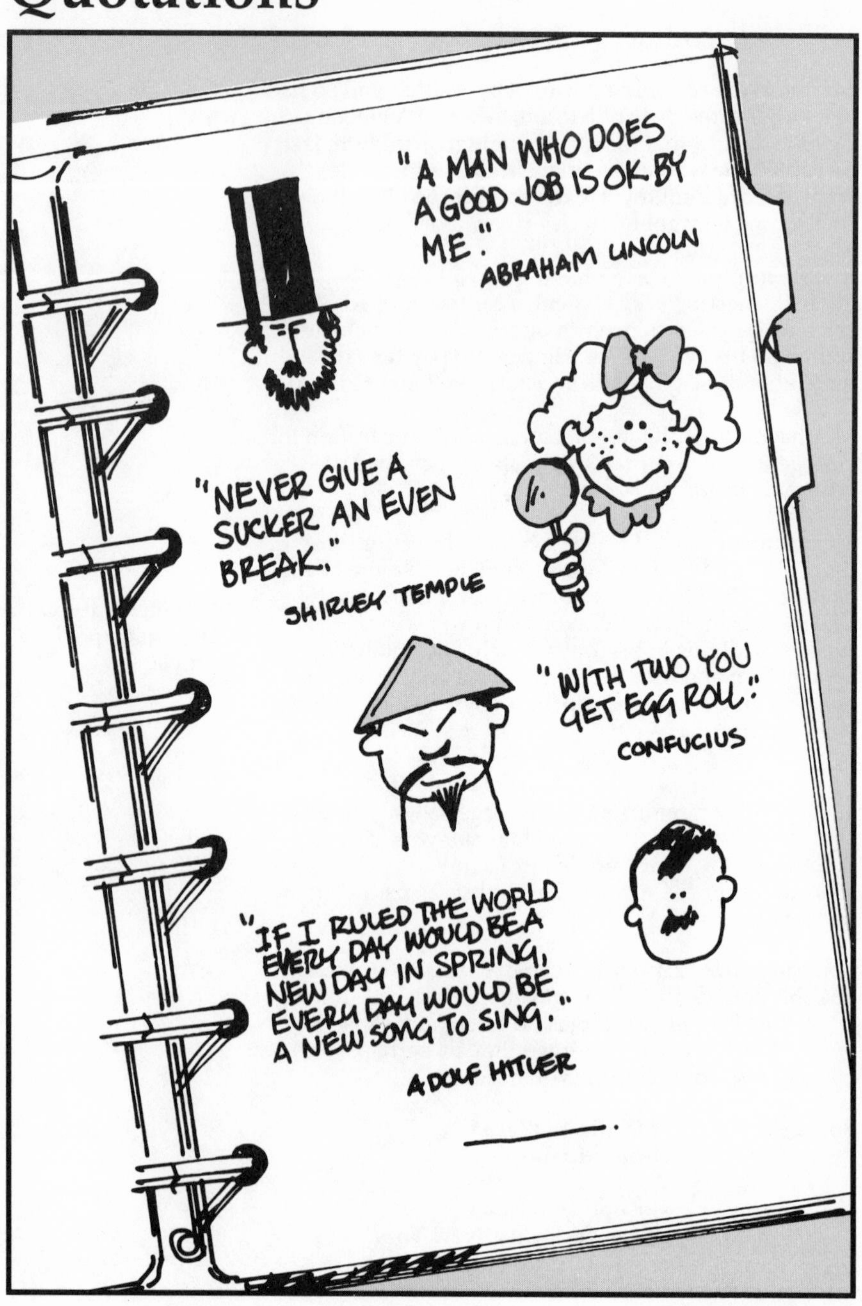

78

You may know that I am a poems-and-sayings fanatic. I love to hear, memorize and share good quotes. Consequently, I receive many letters with sayings in them. These are some of my favorites.

It has been my experience that folks who have no vices have very few virtues.

—Abraham Lincoln

That which we persist in doing becomes easier for us to do; not that the nature of the thing itself is changed, but that our power to do is increased.

—Ralph Waldo Emerson

There is no chance, no destiny, no fate
that can circumvent or hinder or control
the firm resolve of a determined soul.

—Ella Wheeler Wilcox

Every morning in Africa a gazelle wakes up. It knows it must run faster than the fastest lion or it will be killed. Every morning a lion wakes up also. It knows that it must outrun the slowest gazelle or it will starve to death. It doesn't matter whether you are a lion or a gazelle. When the sun comes up you had better be running.

—Unknown

The shadow by my finger cast,
Divides the future from the past.
Behind its unreturning line,
The vanished hour, no longer thine.
Before it lies the unknown hour,
In darkness and beyond thine power.
One hour alone is in thine hands,
The now on which the shadow stands.

—Wellesley College Sundial

This time, like all times, is a very good one, if we but know what to do with it.

—Ralph Waldo Emerson

This is life—and it is passing. What are we waiting for?

—Richard L. Evans

Travel Itinerary Forms

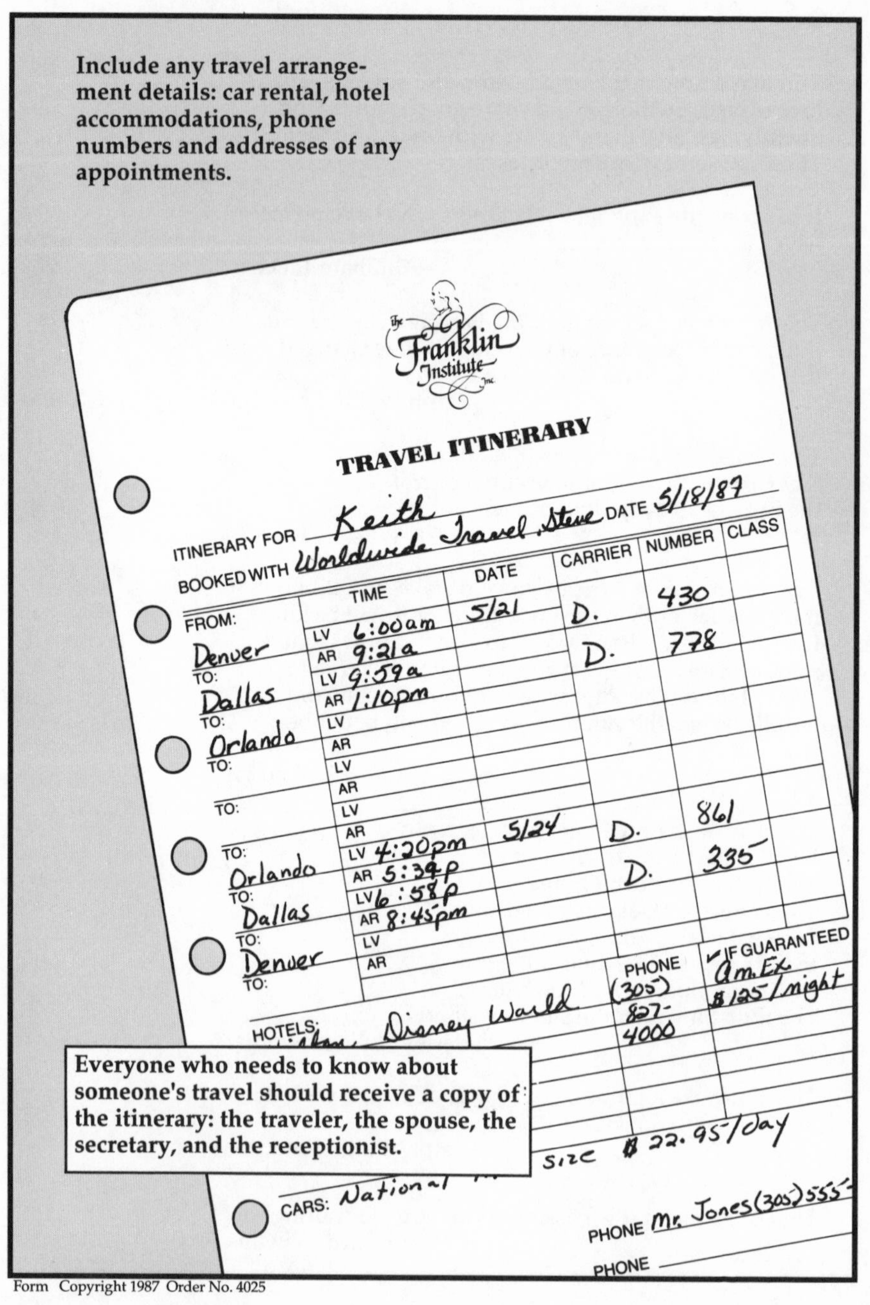

Include any travel arrangement details: car rental, hotel accommodations, phone numbers and addresses of any appointments.

The Franklin Institute Inc.

TRAVEL ITINERARY

ITINERARY FOR Keith DATE 5/18/87

BOOKED WITH Worldwide Travel, Steve

	TIME	DATE	CARRIER	NUMBER	CLASS
FROM: Denver	LV 6:00am	5/21	D.	430	
	AR 9:21a		D.	778	
TO: Dallas	LV 9:59a				
	AR 1:10pm				
TO: Orlando	LV				
	AR				
TO:	LV				
	AR				
TO:	LV				
	AR	5/24	D.	861	
TO: Orlando	LV 4:20pm		D.	335	
	AR 5:39p				
TO: Dallas	LV 6:58p				
	AR 8:45pm				
TO: Denver	LV				
	AR				
TO:					

HOTELS:	PHONE	✓ IF GUARANTEED
Hilton, Disney World	(305) 827-4000	Am.Ex. $125/night

Everyone who needs to know about someone's travel should receive a copy of the itinerary: the traveler, the spouse, the secretary, and the receptionist.

size $22.95/day

CARS: National

PHONE Mr. Jones (305) 555-

PHONE

It was 9:00 on a Monday morning when Keith arrived at the office. His secretary, Marilyn Walters, greeted him and asked if he was ready for his trip. "TRIP? Omigosh, I thought that was next Monday." Marilyn gave him the ticket and sent him flying out the door. An hour later Keith called from the airport. His wife wasn't home, and would Marilyn please call later and tell her where he had gone and when he'd be back. He hadn't had time to leave her a note. Unfortunately, this wasn't unusual. Keith frequently forgot flights, and usually forgot to tell his wife where he was going.

For Christmas, everyone in the office received Franklin Day Planners. Marilyn spotted the Travel Itinerary Forms and ordered some the next day. Now, whenever a trip is planned for Keith, she fills out a Travel Itinerary and makes three copies: one for Keith, one for his wife (Marilyn mails it to her), and one for the receptionist. (She keeps the original for herself.) Keith puts his copy in his Planner between the pages of the day he travels. He also notes on his Monthly Calendar where he is going and what time the plane leaves.

Marilyn writes that the Travel Itinerary has reduced a lot of stress in the office, but the most grateful person is Keith's wife. She appreciates knowing in advance where Keith is going, where he is staying, and how to reach him if she needs to. Marilyn said that this year she received flowers on Secretary's Day from Keith's wife!

Source: **Marilyn Walters**
Denver, Colorado

Advanced Time Management Tip Sheet

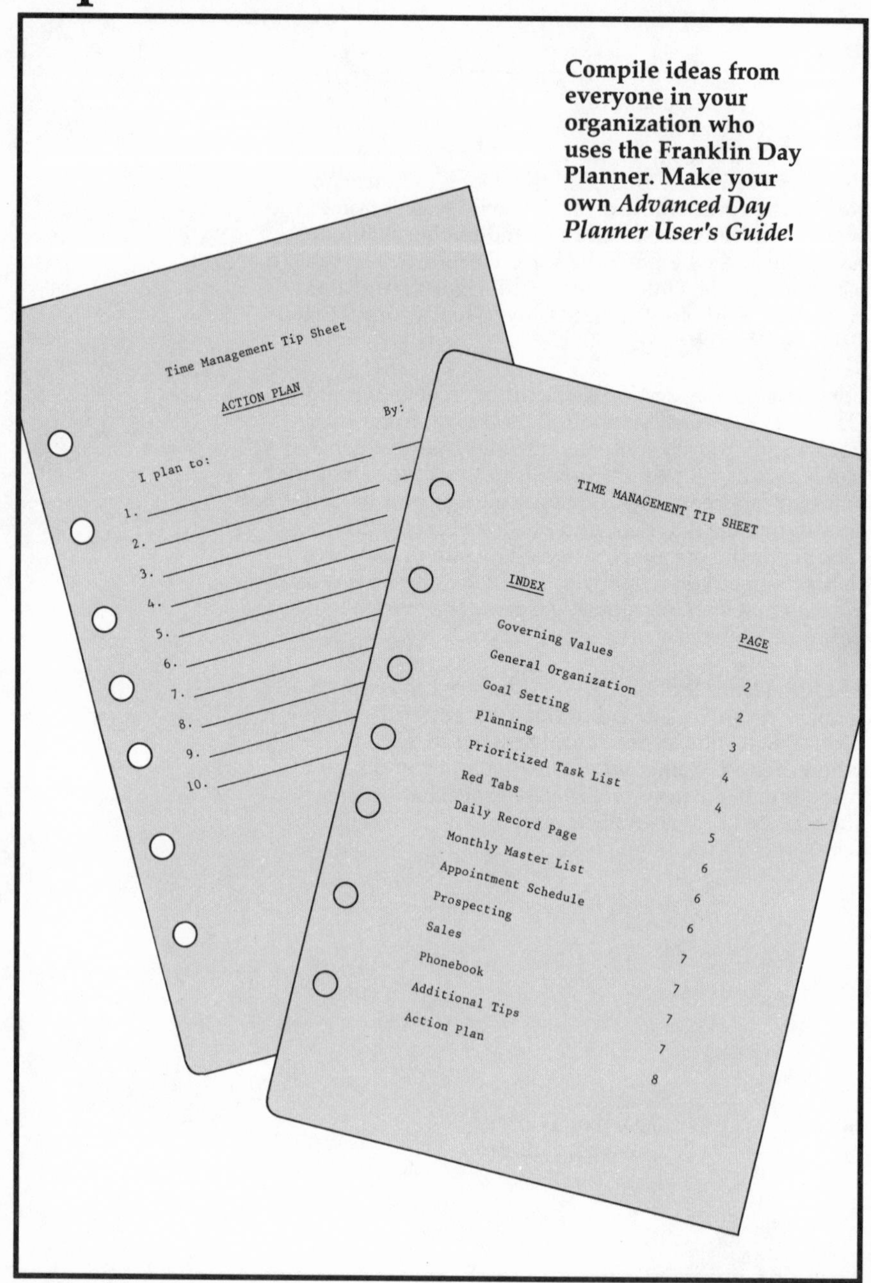

Compile ideas from everyone in your organization who uses the Franklin Day Planner. Make your own *Advanced Day Planner User's Guide*!

Each kind of business requires different procedures and processes. Real estate brokers use the Planner differently than doctors, and managers differently than teachers.

Stan Elson of Merrill Lynch recognized the value of offering training specific to financial consultants' needs; he developed and copyrighted his own Advanced Financial Consultant Training Time Management Tip Sheet. He spoke with a number of consultants who were already using the Franklin Day Planner, and compiled their suggestions into a handy eight-page document. The tips are specifically for financial consultants at Merrill Lynch, and discuss such topics as goal setting, sales and prospecting, planning, using the Red Tabs, and more. The last page of the Tip Sheet is an action plan goal page where individuals can identify the ideas they want to use and set goals for implementing them.

Your company's procedures are different from any other's. Include how to incorporate and coordinate them using the Day Planner.

Each member of the Advanced Financial Consultant Training Program at Merrill Lynch receives a Franklin Day Planner, the Time Management seminar, and Stan's Tip Sheet. The consultants have responded very favorably to the idea. They comment that it helps them to remember principles taught in the seminar, and to coordinate Merrill Lynch procedures with the Planner.

Any organization where many employees are using the Franklin Day Planner can benefit from this kind of customized idea source. The Franklin Institute can help prepare and print it—your company's own *Advanced Day Planner User's Guide*!

Source: **Stan Elson**
Merrill Lynch
Princeton, New Jersey

Daily Goals

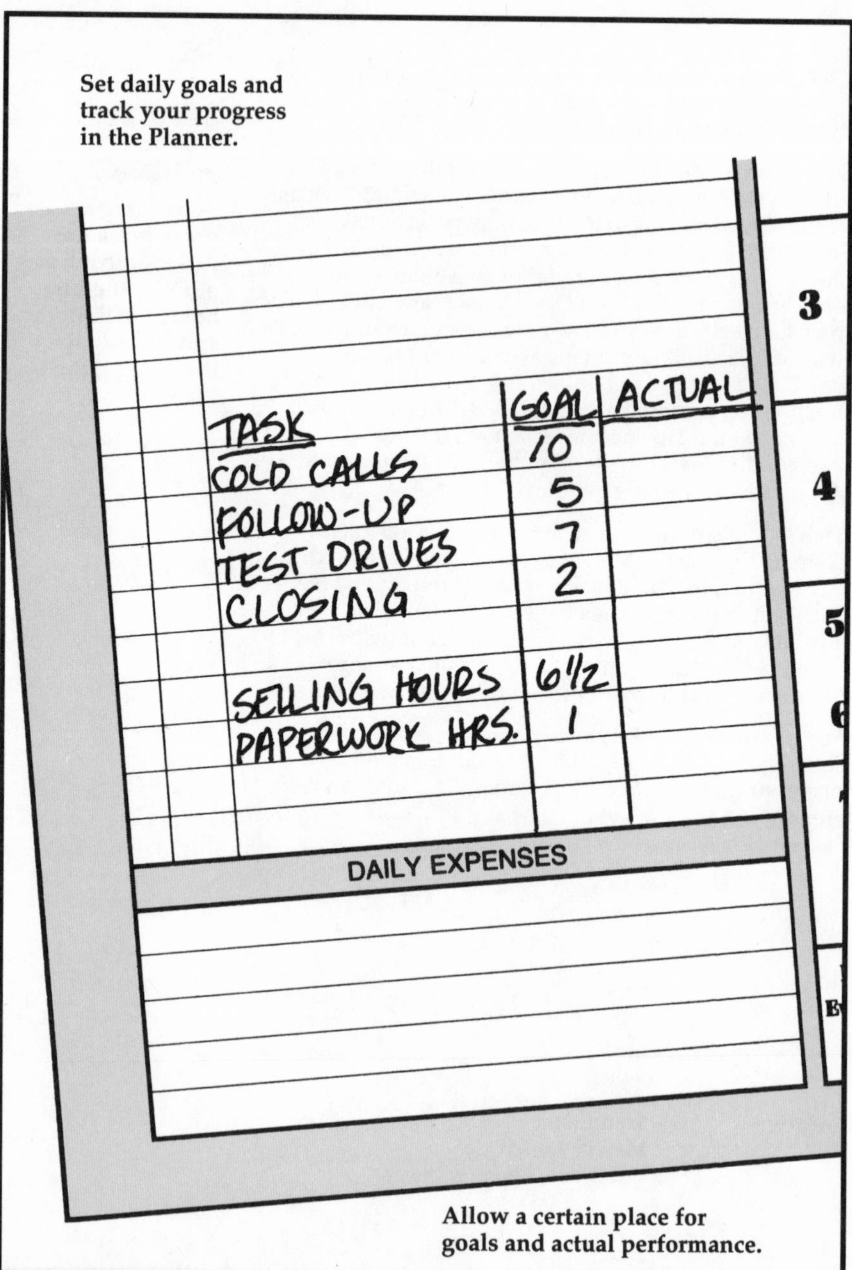

Set daily goals and track your progress in the Planner.
TASK
GOAL
ACTUAL
COLD CALLS
10
FOLLOW-UP
5
TEST DRIVES
7
CLOSING
2
SELLING HOURS
6½
PAPERWORK HRS.
1
DAILY EXPENSES
3
4
5
Allow a certain place for goals and actual performance.

81

On a flight to Midland, Michigan, I once sat next to a man named Bobby Franks, whom I had trained about a year before in a public seminar in Los Angeles. He related to me a very interesting experience.

His first sales position had been at a second-rate used car lot. He didn't do very well and quit. On a whim he answered a want ad for a sales position with training. It turned out to be another used car dealership, but Bobby interviewed anyway. He was offered the job, and accepted on a trial basis—he wasn't sure if this job would be any better than the last one.

Bobby thought the sales training would consist of boring meetings—but he didn't attend a sales meeting for three months. Instead, he was required to account for every minute of the working day. In a one-on-one interview with his boss, Fred, he identified the various activities required in sales: approaches or cold calls, follow-up, asking the right questions, test drives, closing the sale. In a small notebook, he set goals and tallied each of these activities every day. He also recorded the amount of time spent with customers and doing paperwork.

Each week Bobby gave a full report. In these interviews, Fred taught him some sales principles. Soon, his performance was improving significantly. Bobby learned the value (and payoff) of each of the activities he daily tracked. His goals and performance improved almost weekly.

In six months, Bobby was transferred to new car sales. Five years later, working for a prestigious dealership in Beverly Hills, he still sets daily goals and tracks performance and use of time. But now he does it in the Day Planner, in a corner of the Prioritized Daily Task List.

Bobby said that applying the principles taught in our seminar made an even greater difference in his productivity—his sales increased by fifteen percent that year.

Source: **Bobby Franks**
Los Angeles, California

Telephone Log

Records all messages on one page.

Gary

TELEPHONE LOG

DATE	TIME	NAME	*	NUMBER	MESSAGE
7/6	8:20	Dick Jones	✓	(616) 555-1486	returned your call
7/6	10:00	Mary Ann Judd	✓	(316) 999-1585	re: upcoming sem.
7/6	2:00	Liz Shoop	✓	(219) 666-2505	Call
7/6	4:10	Mike Rich	✓	222-1501	needs to meet w/you
7/7	11:15	Bev Wilkinson	✓	(705) 563-3682	re: Company wants to train 1500 emp.
				(601) 981-1111	September sem.
7/7	12:05	Jerry Johnson	R(✓)	(522) 615-1030	interested in trng.
7/7	3:00	Randy Allen	✓	(800) 888-1605	ref. by Dave
7/8	9:00	Rodger Brown	•	(877) 717-6565	flight for 7/25 Sem.
7/8	9:15	Jean Call	R(✓)	(877) 292-2505	interested in Sales
7/9	10:25	Wendy Hall			trng.-Retail

* = Call completed; message answered
✓ = Duplicate message appears later in log
→ = Call deleted; message will not be answered
× = Delegated call; message forwarded to another pa
G(✓) = In process, left return message
● =

Keep one Telephone Log sheet for each person—the white copy goes to the person and the yellow copy stays with the secretary.

Not too long ago, the Marketing Department received a call from a prospective client in Venezuela. Becky Bingham took the message, recorded it on a Telephone Log, and relayed the message to one of the consultants. About a month later, the consultant wanted to call this prospect again and couldn't find his phone number anywhere—he had forgotten to record it in his Prospect File. Becky turned to her file of past Telephone Logs and found the number within minutes.

The Telephone Log is a form for recording several phone calls and messages. Becky keeps one sheet for each person, and gives the messages daily or whenever the person returns to the office or phones in. Gary, her boss, likes the Telephone Log because when he returns from a trip there aren't 25 floating message papers scattered across his desk. Becky likes it because it keeps all calls in one place, and because it makes a copy (on NCR paper) for her own records. In fact, Becky uses it so much that she says, "To love the Telephone Log is to love the Day Planner!"

Source: **Becky Bingham**
The Franklin Institute, Inc.
Salt Lake City, Utah

Daily Affirmations

In the Time Management seminar, I strongly emphasize the importance of writing down values, and setting goals from them. Values and goals should be reviewed often; they keep priorities in focus and give direction to our daily activities.

One woman sent in the following, which she keeps in her Planner and reads every morning. It reflects her values and goals, and daily motivates and uplifts her.

Keep your goals and values in the Planner where you can review them frequently.

> *Realizing the great heritage that is mine, I see myself as a graceful, elegant, attractive, self-confident, and intelligent woman of great worth. . . . I only give advice when asked for.*
>
> *I avoid saying anything to anyone that would discredit my husband's character. I speak well of him.*
>
> *I enjoy eating sensibly. I value proper nutrition. I decide today to eat thin. I use my ability to say "no" when I'm not hungry. . . . I live healthy! . . .*
>
> *Life has been good to me. I have had many rewarding experiences. I accept whatever life unfolds to me. I love life and live it to the fullest. I share the strengths and talents that are uniquely my own. I put my best into each task and leave each situation better than I found it.*

Write values as affirmations, in the present tense.

> *I seek and find that which is beautiful in all people and all things. My heart is full of love and warm with compassion. I find joy in living and peace within myself. . . . I seek charity towards all people, especially my family. I feel energetic, magnificent, and I radiate joy.*
>
> *I am excited about today's challenges. . . . Today is going to go well for me.*
>
> *If I can imagine it, I can achieve it.*
> *If I can dream it, I can become it.*

Here's Your Chance . . .

The Franklin Institute would like to hear your ideas, too. If you want to contribute ideas for a forthcoming *Advanced Day Planner User's Guide, Volume II,* please send them to:

Lisa Vermillion
The Franklin Institute, Inc.
PO Box 25127
Salt Lake City, UT 84125-0127

Index

G

H

I

J

K

L

M

N

O

P

Q

R

S

T

V

W

Z